3703680083

AFTER RELIGION

UNIVERSITY OF
GLOUCESTERSHIRE
at Cheltenham and Gloucester

**FRANCIS CLOSE HALL
LEARNING CENTRE**

Swindon Road Cheltenham
Gloucestershire GL50 4AZ
Telephone: 01242 714600

NORMAL LOAN

2 1 JAN 2011

WITHDRAWN

D1380428

AFTER RELIGION

'Generation X'
and the search for meaning

GORDON LYNCH

FCH LEARNING CENTRE
UNIVERSITY OF GLOUCESTERSHIRE
Swindon Road
Cheltenham GL50 4AZ
Tel: 01242 714600

DARTON·LONGMAN+TODD

To my friends

First published in 2002 by
Darton, Longman and Todd Ltd
1 Spencer Court
140–142 Wandsworth High Street
London SW18 4JJ

© 2002 Gordon Lynch

The right of Gordon Lynch to be identified as the Author
of this work has been asserted in accordance with the
Copyright, Designs and Patents Act 1988.

ISBN 0–232–52429–7

A catalogue record for this book is available from the British Library.

Designed by Sandie Boccacci
Phototypeset in 10/13pt Palatino by Intype London Limited
Printed and bound in Great Britain by
The Bath Press, Bath

CONTENTS

But then I must remind myself we are living creatures – we have religious impulses – we *must* – and yet into what cracks do these impulses flow in a world without religion? It is something I think about every day. Sometimes I think it is the only thing I should be thinking about.

(Douglas Coupland, *Life After God*)

INTRODUCTION

I don't usually get writer's block. But sitting down to write this Introduction has proven to be a hard task for me. I'm not sure how many attempted drafts I've written, though I haven't yet become desperate enough to resort to tidying my office or doing the washing up as an escape from it.

I think what makes this a harder book for me to introduce is that, whilst it is intended to be an academically credible piece of work, it is also quite deeply personal. The themes that I am attempting to address here are very wide-ranging. What is happening to institutional religion within contemporary Western culture? In what ways are people trying to find meaning and purpose in their lives within and beyond organised religion? What represents a healthy or plausible spirituality for our times? Yet despite the breadth and generality of these questions, my desire to ask them is very much driven by my own personal experience. I will say a bit more about that experience later on, but for now it will suffice for me to say that this book emerges very much out of my own struggle to make sense of my life in recent years.

In writing this book, though, my interest has been not only to try to clarify issues that could help me understand my own life but to write a piece of theology that might be helpful more generally to people who are concerned with the pursuit of meaning in contemporary Western culture. Working in the Department of Theology at Birmingham University, I am a recent addition to a long tradition of pastoral and practical theologians who have been fundamentally concerned in their work with trying to help people make sense of their real lived experience. I share the commitment of these colleagues to an approach to theology that begins with our lived experience and tries to explore how we can best understand it or how we might best live in the light of that experience. The experience that forms the starting point of this book is the struggle to achieve a sense of meaning in life that I have felt, and that I also sense in other people whom I meet in different parts of my life. Although this book is necessarily concerned with developing a social and cultural analysis that might help us understand the contemporary context in which our search for meaning takes place, my ultimate intention is for this to lead into more explicitly theological questions. How can we best understand life? What views of life might help us to live more imaginatively, courageously and constructively? What stories, symbols or ideas can help us resist contemporary forces and structures that dehumanise us or starve our spiritual lives? Can the idea of 'God' have any real significance for us any more? I cannot pretend to have achieved anything beyond a cursory or initial discussion of just some of these issues in this book, but my hope is that, even with its inevitable limitations, what follows will be of some value to the on-going discussion of personal meaning in the contemporary world.

Clearly the kind of issues and questions that have led me to write this book are extremely broad. To provide some clearer focus and structure to the following discussion I have chosen to use the notion of 'Generation X' as a central concept. Again this choice partly reflects my personal experience. I first came across the term 'Generation X' through reading Douglas Coupland's novel of the same name. That novel, and other books by Coupland, have been very formative upon me and my own view is that Coupland is a particularly perceptive commentator on the contemporary search for meaning. A central purpose of this book is to attempt to articulate some of the key elements of what I think Coupland has to say about this search. Beyond this, though, my decision to focus on the concept of 'Generation X' reflects my desire to engage critically with the growing literature that attempts to explore 'Generation X' religion or to do 'Generation X' theology. In particular, this book can be read as a response to Tom Beaudoin's *Virtual Faith* (1998) which has become a popular text in this area. As will become clear in what follows, I have very mixed feelings about Beaudoin's work. On one hand, I am hugely grateful to him for focusing attention on the notion of 'Generation X' and for adding strength to the argument that theologians need to take more seriously the ways in which people are making sense of life in contemporary culture outside of organised religion. I also think that Beaudoin is right to draw our attention to the importance of popular culture as a resource in the construction of personal meaning. I am more sceptical, however, about his acceptance of 'generational' definitions of 'Generation X' and of his more specific ideas about the 'religious' significance of popular culture. But all of this will become clearer in due course.

This book is structured in three parts. The first part is concerned with a broad analysis of social and cultural trends in contemporary religion and the individual search for meaning. In chapter 1, I begin with the story of a shift in my own religious beliefs and then go on to explore how my own disengagement from a particular religious tradition seems to reflect wider cultural trends in Britain and the United States. Although institutional religion (certainly in the form of the Christian Church) seems to be in more marked decline in Britain compared to the United States, there seems to be a common trend in both countries of people becoming less committed to particular religious groups or institutions. Instead of this commitment to particular groups, sociological evidence suggests that people are increasingly engaged in a personal pursuit of meaning in a 'spiritual marketplace' that leads them to engage with a range of groups, philosophies and practices, not all of which would traditionally have been thought of as 'religious'. In chapter 2, I then move on to exploring the usefulness of the concept of 'Generation X' for understanding this contemporary search for personal meaning. Much of the literature that talks of 'Generation X' in Western society describes it as a particular generational cohort of people born between the early 1960s and the late 1970s/ early 1980s. In this chapter, I argue that such 'generational' definitions of this term are unhelpful and that it is more useful (and in keeping with the work of Douglas Coupland) to see 'Generation X' rather as a particular attitude than an indication of one's birth-date. In particular I argue that the 'Generation X' view of life is one in which people seek meaning that feels personally authentic to them rather than being prepared to accept 'pre-packaged' truths provided by religious, political or corporate organisations.

In the second part of the book, I then start to look at more specific forms that the 'Generation X' search for meaning might be taking. In chapter 3, there is an exploration of how 'Generation

X' attitudes have become evident within Evangelical Christianity, and I discuss how the notion of the 'post-evangelical' and the growth of 'alternative worship' reflect 'Generation X' concerns. In chapters 4 and 5, the focus turns more to forms that the 'Generation X' search for meaning may be taking outside of institutional religion. In chapter 4, we explore the idea from the American theologian Tom Beaudoin that popular culture can be seen as a set of 'religious texts' that help people to make sense of life. Through a discussion of responses to the film *The Matrix*, it becomes clear in this chapter that whilst popular culture may be a useful resource for helping people think about life, the way in which people interpret and make use of a film like *The Matrix* can be highly diverse and idiosyncratic. Rather than being 'stable' texts that give us a clear view of life, popular cultural texts such as films, pop songs, books and TV programmes can therefore be open to a wide range of uses and interpretations depending on other values, beliefs and commitments that the reader or audience holds. This discussion is carried into chapter 5 which explores whether there might be such a thing as a clubbing spirituality. The use of religious imagery in club culture is explored, and a range of evidence is considered that suggests that the club scene is a source of meaningful experiences for a number of people. Again, though, a closer inspection of the way in which a particular group of people interpret their clubbing experiences shows that whilst they value them highly, they also understand those clubbing experiences quite differently depending on more general values and beliefs that they each individually hold.

In the final part of the book, the focus turns to more explicitly theological questions. In chapter 6, a discussion is offered of possible resources for a 'Generation X' spirituality through a series of reflections on the fiction of Douglas Coupland. Coupland's work provides a clear account of the struggle to achieve a personal sense of meaning and purpose, but he also emphasises the importance of remaining committed to the pursuit of meaning rather than falling into despair or an ironic attitude to life. Coupland's novels suggest that life may not indeed be meaningless and that we may occasionally glimpse sight of its meaning and value through particular momentary (often physical) experiences. Whilst such experiences may not provide us with a grand over-arching theology or philosophy of life, they can at least give us some fragmentary sense that life is valuable, that kindness is possible or that we can be accepted. Finally, in chapter 7, we explore the question of whether the notion of 'God' can have any real significance for the 'Generation X' search for meaning. Three different perspectives on this are set out. Mike Starkey argues that belief in a personal God is the only real hope we have for achieving a stable sense of identity and purpose in a fragmented culture, and that without such a belief we are abandoned to narcissistic, consumerist forms of spirituality. By contrast, Anthony Pinn argues that such traditional theistic beliefs cannot be reconciled with our real experience of the world – in particular, the experience of suffering – and that it is for us to take responsibility for defining the meaning of our lives and living a moral existence. The third view, that of Paul Tillich, is that there is a greater reality in which our individual lives are grounded. Whilst we might use the word 'God' to describe this reality, it ultimately transcends any name or concept that we have for it. Nevertheless, this reality, the 'ground of our being', can break into our awareness at times to give us a sense of greater meaning and value in life. To conclude, some more general observations are made about the significance for religion of the contemporary search for meaning as it has been described in this book.

I am grateful to a number of people who have provided important support and encouragement to me during the writing of this book. It has been a genuine pleasure to have worked with the staff at DLT in the production of this book, and I am particularly grateful to Katie Worrall and Kathy Dyke for all their editorial support. Various colleagues have also given me various forms of help along the way. I am grateful to Paul Heelas, Linda Woodhead and Pete Ward for their encouragement at various times. Conversations with Neil Elliott at different stages of the project have been hugely valuable to me. Material provided by Jonny Baker was also very useful. In my own department, Robert Beckford and Martin Stringer have been particularly helpful to me with this project. And, as ever, Stephen Pattison has been a very encouraging and engaging conversation-partner. I used some of the ideas in this book in my teaching on the Religion in Contemporary Britain module as part of the BA in Theology at Birmingham University. My thanks to Emma Heathcote-James for working with me on that and for her infectious enthusiasm for this subject. I am also very grateful for the conversations with students on that course which encouraged me to pursue this material further and which developed my own thinking on it. A couple of the chapters in the book were also presented as seminars at the 'Critical Mass' event held at St Luke's, Holloway in April 2001, and I am grateful for the feedback from participants as well as the invitation from Dave and Pat Tomlinson to be part of that.

Various parts of the book were read by Matthew Guest, Steve Taylor and Sarah White. I am hugely grateful to them for their thoughts and comments about my work. Without their feedback and encouragement this would be a weaker and less fluent text. Any remaining flaws are my responsibility alone.

I wish to thank the following individuals for permission to use internet-based material for this book: Chris Bullivant on behalf of Soul Survivor, Cecil Copeland for Awesomehouse.com, Sid Galloway for Soulcare.org, Jake Horsley for Wynd.org, and Adrian Riley for Host. Being able to use this material has been very beneficial for the following discussion and I am very grateful to all of them.

Finally, one of the parts of this book that I ended up cutting out was a short section on the importance of friendship (that will have to wait for another day). Ray Pahl (2001) has written that friendship seems to be emerging as one of the most important structures in providing us with some continuity and security in our fragmented and transient culture. The last year has been the most challenging of my adult life to date, and I know that my survival is largely down to the friends who have been there with me through it. I am indebted to many people, but especially to John, Kathryn, Steve, Marie, Derek, Tracey, Roger, Manda, David, Stephen, Sue, Sarah, Susannah, Bella, Alan, Robert, Marion, Cindy, Steve, Nic, Pete, Barbara, John and Jan. My thanks go out to all of you, and it is to you that this book is dedicated.

GORDON LYNCH
Department of Theology, University of Birmingham
February 2002

1
After Religion?

Let me begin with a confession. I used to be an Evangelical Christian. I believed in the Bible as the ultimate Word of God and of the importance of being personally saved by Jesus. I was an enthusiastic member of churches in which the idea that God supernaturally heals people was taken as read, in which speaking in tongues was not uncommon, and in which many people took seriously the idea of demonic influences in the world. In my teenage years and early twenties I regularly took part in Bible-study discussions and had earnest conversations about the potential sinfulness of a range of activities from gay relationships, smoking, swearing, masturbation and listening to certain kinds of pop music. And it would usually turn out that a range of lifestyles or activities that did not fit neatly into the circumscribed beliefs and ethics of my church were indeed sinful.

Now this might not seem to be a very promising opening to a book. For some readers who are Evangelical Christians, the fact that I am no longer one myself may make me a somewhat suspicious or possibly 'unsound' author. For other readers without a background in Evangelical Christianity, the fact that I spent my formative years engaged in activities and discussions that may well just appear quite wacky, may not make me seem that credible either.

In actual fact, though, I think the fact that I have changed from being a committed Evangelical Christian to someone who would no longer regard themselves as Christian, whilst still at the same time having sympathies for some Christian beliefs, is an important basis for writing this book. Partly this is because I think that my experience of moving away from a clear Christian faith and from committed membership of the Church is not at all unique. When I was an undergraduate student most of the people I spent time with were committed Christians. When I look at that peer-group now, I see that most of them have little or no connection with the Church any more and that their religious beliefs bear little relation to what they believed fifteen years ago. The popularity of Dave Tomlinson's book *The Post-Evangelical* (1995) (to which we will return in chapter 3) further suggests that there is a substantial number of people who are disillusioned with the kind of rigid Christianity that I grew up with, and who are trying to find new ways of making sense of their lives.

Quite how I came to abandon my Evangelical beliefs is a long story, and one that is perhaps better told on another occasion. One of the effects of my own personal religious de-conversion, though, is to make me more aware of the declining influence of Christianity in Western culture more generally. When I was part of the Evangelical sub-culture (with its specialised books, films, music, celebrities, and so on), it was easy to believe that Christianity still had an important role in society. When I stepped outside of that sub-culture, however, I began to realise how unimportant Christianity and the Church is now to many people in the West. Furthermore, I began to realise (ashamed as I am to admit this) that a wide range of different beliefs and lifestyles that I had been suspicious of in the past actually had genuine integrity to them.

This possibly rather peculiar-sounding late introduction to mainstream Western culture has had one very useful effect on me. It has left me profoundly curious about how people in Western society make sense of their lives, and what values and beliefs are important to them, given that formal religion seems to play little part in their lives. Partly this curiosity relates to myself. How do I make sense of my life now that I have stepped outside of a clear set of religious ideas and beliefs? But I am also curious about us all in Western society. Is it important for us to find some meaning in life? And if so, how do we go about doing that? These are the kind of questions that have motivated me to write this book.

This personal introduction may still leave some readers a bit suspicious. Is this really just an exercise in academic navel-gazing in which I am projecting my own religious doubts and struggles onto wider society? You may be relieved to know that I don't think that this is in fact the case. In this first chapter, then, we will spend some time examining the evidence that institutional religion (in particular the Christian Church) may be commanding a much less important role in our lives than for previous generations and that individuals' search for meaning in life may be taking increasingly diverse forms. Initially, we will do this by exploring the state of the institutional Church in Britain before comparing this to the situation in the United States and making some more general observations.

The case of the disappearing Church – institutional religion in Britain

The Christian Church in Britain is going through an extra-ordinary period of change. The rapidly declining rates in church attendance lead some sociologists to suggest that it is entering a phase of near-terminal decline from which it is unlikely ever to recover to any significant extent. Consider the following predictions from the British sociologist, Steve Bruce:

> By 2030, mainstream Christianity in Britain will have largely disappeared. Total Christian Church membership will be below 5% as will church attendance. If it has not already merged with the Church of England, British Methodism will die in 2031 and other denominations will be close behind. 50% of funerals will still have some sort of vaguely religious ceremony, but fewer than 10% of babies will be baptised or marriages celebrated in church. The % of people describing themselves as Christian will be below 20. Even in its most vague form, less than half of us will say that we believe in God; more than half of us will say we do not.
>
> The dominant form of religion, insofar as we have any, will be the thoroughly individualistic therapeutic solipsistic religion of the cultic world of New Age spirituality. But it will have very little salience even for those who claim to embrace it.

> In short, the United Kingdom in 2030 will be an obviously
> secular society.[1]

Bruce argues for the validity of these predictions on the basis of statistical trends that chart a steady decline in organised religion in Britain over the past forty years. His suggestion that less than 5 per cent of the British population will attend church regularly in thirty years' time is therefore a figure projected from current declining numbers within the Church. Whilst, of course, we cannot assume that church attendance figures will continue to fall at a steady rate, there does seem to be some good evidence to support Bruce's predictions. Indeed the most recent major survey of church attendance in Britain has highlighted two particular trends that suggest further numerical decline for the British Church (see Brierley, 1999).

Firstly, the number of people attending church fell at a faster rate between 1989 and 1998 than it did between 1979 and 1989.[2] With the decline in numbers of those regularly attending church beginning to accelerate, and with only 7.5 per cent of the English population regularly attending church in 1998, Steve Bruce's prediction that less than 5 per cent of people in Britain will attend church regularly in 2030 does not look too implausible. Secondly, the United Kingdom church attendance survey also indicated that the numbers of those who attend church regularly are increasingly made up of people over sixty-five, and that the number of children attending church is dramatically decreasing. Between 1989 and 1998 the percentage of the church population aged 65 or over grew from 19 per cent to 25 per cent, and over that same period of time the church population aged fifteen or under fell from 25 per cent to 19 per cent.[3] In demographic terms, then, the church population is an ageing one, and we have now reached the point where the numbers of church members who die in the coming years will not be replaced by equal numbers of new members coming into the church in childhood.

These statistics suggest, then, that Steve Bruce may well be correct to predict an ongoing decline in the numbers of people attending church in the coming years. Regardless of whether this decline continues at the rate that he suggests, however, Bruce is already sceptical about the significance of institutional religion in Britain today. He writes:

> There is very widespread agreement that Britain's religious life is not what it used to be. Although not regarded with any great hostility, our churches are unpopular, their teachings are ignored by the vast majority of the population, their leaders no longer have the ears of our rulers, their efforts to glorify God are barely noticed, and their beliefs no longer inform the presuppositions of the wider culture . . . Many of those who continue to attend to the supernatural are oriented, not to an external God and his writ over the world and all it contains, but to the inner self. There are enclaves where religion remains potent – where it is closely associated with a threatened ethnic identity, where its adherents have isolated themselves from the mainstream, and where it aids ethnic minorities in coming to terms with their place in a new world – but they are only enclaves. In so far as the supernatural or the spiritual is still to be found in the mainstream, it is in almost homeopathic concentrations: so watered down as to be a shadow of its former self, nearly undetectable to the untrained eye. (Bruce, 1995, p. 125)

Whilst Steve Bruce has a pessimistic view of the future status of religion in Britain, other writers have suggested that his degree of pessimism is unwarranted and represents only a partial reading of our current situation. Another leading sociologist of religion in Britain, Grace Davie, offers a very contrasting account of British religious life and sees religious faith as still a significant force within our culture.

In her writing Davie has been keen to argue against the idea that Britain is increasingly secularised, if we define a secular society as one in which people tend to think about life in terms of what is scientifically observable rather than with any reference to the supernatural.

Davie's argument seems well supported by a range of evidence that suggests the persistence of religious faith and experiences in contemporary society. Recent surveys of religious belief in Britain have consistently shown that the majority of respondents believe in God or some force or power beyond themselves. A

MORI survey carried out in the United Kingdom in 1998 indicated that 64 per cent of respondents claimed to believe in God
and in a similar survey carried out in 1999 this figure was 71
per cent (see MORI 2001a, 2001b). Such surveys also typically
indicate that significant numbers hold related religious beliefs.
Thus in the 1998 MORI poll 54 per cent of people stated that
they believed in heaven, and in the 1999 poll this figure rose to
58 per cent. In the 1999 poll, 60 per cent of respondents said that
they believed that Jesus was the Son of God. Similarly in a poll
conducted for BBC Online in 2000, 34 per cent of respondents
stated that they prayed at least once a week (MORI, 2001c). By
contrast, however, the numbers of people who report in these
surveys that they are convinced atheists remains comparatively
very small. Davie reports that in the European Values Study
conducted in 1990, only 4.4 per cent of respondents described
themselves as atheists (Davie, 1994, p. 79). In the 1998 MORI
poll, 21 per cent of respondents said they had no religious
affiliations, and the same response was given by only 17 per cent
and 15 per cent of people in the polls conducted by MORI in
1999 and 2000 respectively. The results from surveys of religious
belief in Britain thus suggest that a thoroughly secular view
of the world – in which the notions of God and the supernatural
have no part to play – seems in fact a minority one amongst
individuals in contemporary British society.

Further evidence of the persistence of some form of religious
life in Britain is also provided by research that highlights in
more detailed ways various religious or spiritual experiences
that individuals and groups have had. One of the leading
researchers in this field in Britain is David Hay, who has been
involved in studying spiritual experiences for nearly thirty years.
In a substantial survey conducted in 1976, Hay found that around
a third of his respondents stated that they had had some experience of a presence or power (whether called God or not) that
was different to their everyday selves (Hay, 1982). In a similar
survey conducted in 1986, this figure rose to nearly half of the
people included in the study (Hay, 1990). Evidence of the persistence of spiritual or supernatural experiences has also been
recently provided by research conducted at Birmingham University by Emma Heathcote-James. Heathcote-James (2001) used

adverts in national newspapers to ask people to write to her describing any experience that they had had of encountering an angel, and she has since received over 800 written responses. The degree of wider interest in her research is also indicated by the fact that it gained national and international media coverage from radio stations in New Zealand to *Cosmopolitan* magazine.

Taken together, these kinds of studies of contemporary religious beliefs and experiences suggest that religion and spiritual experience may be far from dead in contemporary Britain. Davie herself recognises the apparent contradiction between research findings that indicate that church attendance is in significant decline and research that indicates that significant numbers of people do still retain religious beliefs and still have spiritual experiences. Davie attempts to reconcile these conflicting findings by arguing for the importance of what she calls 'common religion' in contemporary Britain. 'Common religion' in Britain, Davie argues, represents a broad spectrum of religious beliefs and experiences (often with some connection to the Christian tradition) with which most people identify to some degree. She comments:

> The content of common religion may well, at one end of the spectrum, have some link to Christian teaching. At the other it is enormously diverse, ranging through a wide range of distinctly heterodox ideas: for example ... healing, the paranormal, fortune telling, fate and destiny, life after death, ghosts, spiritual experiences, luck and superstition. (Davie, 1994, p. 83)

Common religion does not therefore very closely resemble orthodox Christian belief (though may well involve beliefs or symbols drawn from it), and it is likely to include a diverse range of attitudes, experiences and practices that vary from person to person. Whilst such common religion may actually be a significant element in people's lives, Davie argues that it does not generally motivate people to become committed members of particular churches or other religious institutions. Religious life in contemporary Britain is therefore characterised, to use Davie's neat phrase, by 'believing without belonging'.

Davie's work does call into question whether Steve Bruce is

right to be so pessimistic about the future of religion in Britain. More specifically, it also raises the issue of whether measurements of church attendance are the best gauge of assessing the state of religion in Britain. For if she is right to suggest that we live in a religious milieu of 'believing without belonging', then it is possible that religious beliefs and attitudes can still be a potent force within our society even though church numbers are falling.

At the same time, however, Bruce (1996) raises some important questions about Davie's ideas. In particular, he asks whether we can actually build much out of surveys that indicate that substantial numbers of people still claim to believe in God. Bruce draws an analogy here between religious faith and supporting a football team. If individuals claim to support a particular football team, but never go to watch a game, do not follow their results or know who any of their players are, then we may begin to doubt how significant their support of that team really is to them. Similarly, Bruce argues, if individuals claim to believe in God, but do not participate in religious services, do not accept (or even know) key religious doctrines, and if their espoused belief does not have any significant impact on the way in which they live, then we may question how significant their claim to religious belief really is.

There is some reasonable evidence to support Bruce's suspicion that respondents' claims to believe in God in surveys do not necessarily represent evidence of significant religious attitudes. For whilst surveys do consistently return high percentages of people claiming to believe in God there are a number of counter-indications within these same surveys that suggest that traditional religious belief is not a significant force in the lives of these respondents. For example, in a 'Millennium poll' conducted by MORI in 1999, 62 per cent of people said that the religious aspect of the Millennium was either not very significant or not at all significant for them, though in the same survey 71 per cent had said that they believed in God. In their poll by BBC Online in 2000, MORI found that only 22 per cent of people said that religion was one of the most significant factors in teaching them right from wrong, way behind one's parents or one's personal experience. In the same poll, only 1 per cent of respondents saw Jesus Christ as a personally inspirational figure, whilst 6 per cent named the singer Britney Spears. Furthermore, in a MORI poll in 1998, people were asked about other elements that Davie associates with common religion such as astrology, tarot-reading, the belief in reincarnation and faith-healing. Typically only around a third to a quarter of all respondents said that they believed in these and, even more significantly, usually less than 20 per cent of those people who believed in them said that they had any influence on decisions they made about their lives.

A comparison of Bruce's and Davie's work thus brings into sharp focus some key issues in the discussion about the state of religion in contemporary Britain. Steve Bruce would seem to be clearly correct in asserting that religious institutions face a serious numerical decline in their membership from which they may never fully recover. Furthermore, Bruce may also be right to suggest that (whilst people may claim to have religious beliefs or experiences) modern forms of rationality tend to be a more significant basis on which people build decisions about their lives. At the same time, though, Davie highlights that the declining numbers of people attending religious services cannot be assumed to indicate that religious beliefs and experiences are completely disappearing from our culture. Indeed, from her perspective, religion in Britain today may be more evident at the level of individuals' beliefs and experiences than through individuals choosing to commit themselves strongly to particular religious groups or institutions. Taken together, their work suggests that institutional religion in Britain (at least in the form of the Christian Church) is in serious decline, but that individuals continue to have a need or desire for personal meaning that may or may not make use of religious ideas or symbols. Whilst there are important differences in this account of religion in Britain today to the current situation with religion in the United States, there are also some important similarities and we shall now turn briefly to look at these.

Towards a 'spiritual marketplace' – religion in contemporary America

One of the most immediately striking differences between religion in contemporary Britain and America is that participation in organised religion seems much higher in the United States. As we have seen, church attendance in Britain currently stands at around 7.5 per cent of the total British population, yet in America polls over the past decade have consistently shown that between 39–48 per cent of respondents say that they attend church or synagogue weekly or nearly every week (Gallup, 2002). A number of other survey responses also suggest that religious belief is seen as an important part of life for a large number of Americans. For example, in an American poll in 2001, 63 per cent of respondents said that they believed religion could answer all or most of life's problems (Gallup, 2002). As with such surveys in Britain, however, we need to be cautious about how we interpret these results. There has been, for example, an interesting discussion about whether the number of Americans who claim to attend church or synagogue regularly in Gallup polls actually far exceeds the numbers who do attend. Indeed, some limited studies which have physically counted the number of people actually attending religious services have suggested that this may amount to as little as 20 per cent of the American population (see Marler and Chaves, 1993; Caplow *et al.*, 1998; Marler and Hadaway, 1999). If this is the case (or even partly true) then it remains interesting that Americans should feel that they need to over-report the number of times they attend religious services to researchers. It has already been commented on by researchers that, when responding to surveys, people tend to overestimate how much they give to charity and that men tend to exaggerate the number of sexual partners that they have had (Walsh, 2002). If Americans similarly tend to overestimate how often they attend church or synagogue because they believe it is a good thing to claim to do then at the very least this reflects an awareness on their part that religion still plays some important role in life. It is difficult to imagine people in Britain wanting to exaggerate their religious observance to the same degree.

Even if attendance at religious services may not be quite as high as Gallup polls indicate, it seems clear that religious beliefs, language and practices remain important to a large number of Americans. Indeed there has been a remarkable continuity in the number of Americans who claim to believe in God, attend religious services regularly and engage in other religious activities (such as prayer or Bible study) since the close of the Second World War (Marty, 1998). Despite the superficial appearance of stability in American religion, however, a growing number of sociologists are suggesting that a profoundly significant change is taking place in the way in which many Americans are now approaching their religious lives. This change is described by the sociologist Wade Clark Roof as a move towards American (and global) culture becoming a 'spiritual marketplace' (Roof, 1999). Following the work of Martin Marty, Roof argues that Americans have historically tended to draw a significant sense of identity from the particular religious group or denomination to which they belonged, and sought to follow the particular beliefs and authority structure of that group. Having conducted extensive interview-based research since 1988, Roof suggests that in the closing years of the twentieth century there has been a noticeable weakening of the commitment that Americans feel towards particular religious institutions. Instead, he notes, Americans increasingly see themselves as engaged in a personal pursuit of meaning, a search that may lead them to engage with different religious groups and traditions as they pursue a religious perspective on life that feels personally meaningful and authentic (see also Porterfield, 2001).

Thus, whilst Americans seem to be engaging with traditional religious beliefs and practices to a greater degree than their British counterparts, a similar trend appears evident within American and British religious life. This is a trend away from people being committed members of particular religious groups or denominations and of them drawing their identity from the particular teachings and practices of that group. Instead, on both sides of the Atlantic, the trend seems to be towards people pursuing religious ideas of life that are personally meaningful and which may draw on a range of different religious traditions or indeed none. People appear to be acting less as observant and dutiful members of religious institutions, and more as 'spiritual seekers' engaged in a search for ways of thinking about and approaching life that seem personally authentic and helpful.

On current evidence, it seems that people in Britain are less likely to engage with the Church as part of their spiritual search than people in America. But there are some limited indications that the American search for meaning may also take place increasingly outside of the Church in the future as well. For example, we noted earlier that there is a debate about the accuracy of the figures for the proportion of the American population that regularly attends religious services. If the real level of attendance at religious services is closer to 20 per cent than 40 per cent, this would lead us to be more cautious about the significance of regular participation in formal religious worship for individual Americans' spiritual searching. It would also seem that commitment to religious institutions is weaker amongst younger adults in America in comparison to adults over the age of sixty-five, with roughly half as many younger adults reporting regular religious attendance as compared to those in later life (Gallup, 2002a). Similarly, in a 1999 survey of American teenagers who regularly attended church, only one in three of the respondents anticipated that they would still be involved in church life when they were older and living by themselves (Barna, 2002). This would seem to match trends in Britain for younger adults, in general, to be less engaged with religious institutions than adults in mid or later life, a trend that suggests a future drop in membership for American religious groups.

Given the historical and cultural significance of religious faith in America it is difficult, at this stage, to envisage the same degree of institutional religious decline that we are witnessing in Britain. The sheer size and cultural diversity of the United States also makes it difficult to make any sensible predictions about future trends in American religious life. Nevertheless, it seems plausible at this point to suggest that Americans are becoming less committed to particular religious groups and denominations and more committed to their own personal spiritual search. Furthermore, this search is one in which they may engage with a range of different religious groups and traditions, as well as beliefs and practices that lie beyond what we may have usually thought of as religious such as alternative health, psychotherapy and personal development workshops.

And so . . .? Exploring a new religious horizon

It would appear, then, that despite its idiosyncrasies the story about my own religious experience at the beginning of this chapter may actually be representative of wider cultural movements. From our very brief discussion of trends in the religious life of Britain and America, a common theme has emerged of individuals' weakening commitment to religious institutions and of an emerging sense of the importance of the personal pursuit of meaning. This theme seems similarly reflected in my own story in which I moved from looking for religious meaning within the confines of a particular religious institution and tradition, towards a pursuit of meaning that was open to a wider range of perspectives and lifestyles.

Now if it is indeed the case that we are seeing a major shift in the way in which people in Western culture are engaging (or not engaging) with religious institutions, and that increasing energy is being placed within Western society on the pursuit of personal meaning, then this raises a number of fundamental questions. Firstly, how can we best understand and describe the changes that are taking place in contemporary Western religion? What theoretical concepts help us to understand how people experience and approach life in contemporary Western society? How are religious institutions and traditions being influenced by these cultural changes? Secondly, if the pursuit of personal meaning in Western society is taking place outside of formal, institutional religion as much as within it, then where are people looking to find meaning? And in what ways do they make use of different cultural and religious resources to express what they believe to be valuable and meaningful in life? Thirdly, from a theological perspective, what kind of resources (stories, symbols, ideas, practices) can be genuinely helpful to us in our contemporary search for meaning? What represents a healthy spirituality for our age, and does 'God' have any significant role to play in it?

These are huge and complex questions, but I believe they represent the most significant questions currently faced by the study of the sociology of Western religion or contemporary theology. More importantly, though, these questions are central for all of us who are trying to live in a meaningful way in contemporary Western culture. These questions, and this book, is therefore not at all meant just for academics, but is intended primarily to stimulate wider debate and reflection on the nature of the contemporary search for meaning and what might help us in that search.

After Religion is part of a growing literature on the nature of religion and the pursuit of meaning in contemporary Western society. Whilst this book could be understood in terms of more general discussions of the significance of 'late' or 'post' modernity for institutional and personal forms of religion (see, e.g., Lyon, 2000; Woodhead and Heelas, 2000), it also fits into a more specific range of books that explore the significance of the concept of 'Generation X' for contemporary religion and spirituality.

As I discuss in more detail in chapter 2, I first encountered the term 'Generation X' through reading Douglas Coupland's novel of the same name. This novel, as well as Coupland's later fiction, have had a significant influence on my work and life more generally. The approach that I adopt in this book therefore reflects my assumption that Coupland is someone who has been able to write about the contemporary search for meaning in particularly perceptive and helpful ways. A fundamental aim of this book is therefore to try to articulate what it is in Coupland's writing that I believe is so useful for helping understand our current situation in Western culture. Quite who or what 'Generation X' is, and what I think Coupland really has to say about this, will be the focus of the next chapter.

2
Will the Real 'Generation X' Please Stand Up?

GenXers are the 80 million Americans who were born between 1961 and 1981. (Flory and Miller, 2000, p. 3)

[I]t's still a good policy to continue defying labels. Once people think they've pigeonholed you, they'll also think they can exploit and use you . . . Refuse to participate in all generational debates. (Coupland, 1995)

A few years ago, someone lent me a copy of Douglas Coupland's novel *Generation X* (1992). I can't remember now why I was interested in reading it – maybe I was strangely drawn by its lurid pink cover. But as I began to read I had a remarkable experience. A newspaper I look at from time to time has a regular column in which people talk about books that have changed their lives. Well, it would be going too far to say that this novel changed my life. But as I read it I began to feel very strongly, and for the first time since I had moved away from my Evangelical Christian roots, that here was someone who understood how I felt about life. Coupland was describing the world in exactly the way that I experienced it. Andy, Claire and Dag, the central characters in *Generation X*, are all rootless and adopt an ironic approach to life whilst at the same time being concerned with trying to make sense of it. Here were characters with whom I could very much identify.

Excited by my reading of this novel, I began to read Coupland's other work, and in it I found the recurring theme of the importance and difficulty of trying to find meaning in the contemporary world (see Coupland, 1994; 1998; 2000; 2001). The title and content of his later novel *Life After God* seemed particularly poignant to me. I also began to realise that I was not alone in my interest in Coupland's work, and that his novels consistently achieved best-seller status in Britain and North America. More recently, I have become aware that Coupland's idea of 'Generation X' is attractive to other people in my academic field as well, as a growing number of books have begun to emerge about the shape of 'Generation X' religion and how the Church should seek to 'reach out' to 'Generation X'.

Over time, though, I have become increasingly convinced that as the number of books about 'Generation X' has grown, so has the degree of misunderstanding about what Coupland meant when he originally coined this phrase. Indeed the fact that Coupland himself has gone on record to advocate abandoning the term 'Generation X' altogether should make us think that something has gone wrong with this as an idea at some point along the road. I still believe, however, that what Douglas Coupland originally meant by the term 'Generation X' is still very helpful as a concept for helping us to understand the contemporary search for meaning in our society. So in this chapter I will take time, first of all, to describe how other writers have used the term 'Generation X'. Then I will try to explain why I think, to a lesser or greater extent, most of these writers misunderstand it. Finally, I will set out what I believe Coupland actually meant when he coined the phrase 'Generation X' in a way that will serve as a basis for our discussions in all the remaining chapters.

Defining a new generation

Since the publication of Douglas Coupland's novel *Generation X* in America in 1991, there has been a growing literature to suggest that within Western society there is a new generation of young people that is characterised by certain common traits, experiences and attitudes. Much of this literature has come from the United States, where in addition to being called 'Generation X', this new generation has also been referred to as the 'baby-busters' (or simply 'busters'). The term 'baby-buster' is used to refer to the fact that this generation followed after the baby boom that took place immediately after the Second World War. Thus people born between 1945 and the early 1960s, in which the birth rate was exceptionally high, are often referred to as 'baby-boomers' or 'boomers', and those born from the 1960s onwards when the birth rate began to fall, are referred to as 'baby-busters' (see Roof, 1988).

Changing patterns in birth rates are arguably not that significant in themselves, but a number of writers have claimed that the 'Generation X' or 'buster' generation has shared a common set of experiences that have profoundly shaped the way in which members of this generation view the world (see, e.g., Howe and Strauss, 1993; Holtz, 1995; Starkey, 1997; Beaudoin, 1998; Cox, 1998; Reifschneider, 1999; Flory and Miller, 2000). For example, Mahedy and Bernadi state that:

> Generation X is the most aborted of America's generations. It suffered the highest parental divorce rate – twice the rate faced by Boomers. Half of all marriages now end in divorce. One in four children is born to a single mother. As they grew to maturity, the second leading cause of death among Xers (after auto accidents) became homicide, followed by suicide.
>
> Generation X was born during the turmoil of Vietnam. Their introduction to politics took place in the Watergate-Irangate era of overt lies and deceit. The second generation raised on television, they have known the mass media only in their more manipulative and trivialised phase. Their exposure to educational systems took place at a time of national decline in school's ability to teach effectively . . .
>
> They live with the very realistic expectation that something bad will probably happen to them. They know that life is hostile and dangerous. They have been abandoned. They are alienated. They are alone. (Mahedy and Bernadi, 1994, pp. 30–2)

This sense of 'Generation X' as a social group that has grown up facing adversity[1] is picked up by a number of other writers. The back cover to Geoffrey Holtz's *Welcome to the Jungle: The 'Why'*

Behind Generation X, expresses this notion of a put-upon generation very clearly:

> Holtz shows exactly how our generation got shafted. But instead of whining about vague problems (as we Xers are so often accused of doing), he whips out the charts and graphs that prove his point: while adults were busy with the social revolution of the 60s and 70s, they plunked us kids in front of the TV, or doped us on Ritalin, or stuck us in prison, or let us languish in poverty. (Holtz, 1995)

Holtz also refers to 'Generation X' as the generation that raised itself, reflecting the notion of this as a generation of latchkey kids left to look after their own upbringing whilst their parent or parents held full-time jobs (see also Beaudoin 1998, p. 21). A further trial that some writers have identified is an economic downturn which means that as 'Generation X' approach adulthood they are the first generational cohort for a number of generations who realistically face more limited job prospects and lower incomes than their parents (Coupland, 1992, pp. 209–11; Flory and Miller, 2000).

Although members of 'Generation X' have faced particular relational and social instability in their formative years of growing up, as well as poor prospects for their future, some writers are keen to emphasise the positive and distinctive qualities that this group has developed as a response to these adversities. Mike Starkey, for example, writes that:

> Xers are more likely to value relationships above success, community above fixed goals, personal authenticity above achievement. Xers are not so much a 'me' generation as a 'we' generation. Boomers still tend to have a touching faith that science and technology will solve our problems. Busters know they never will, and could even make the problems worse. If Boomers have some residual trust in historic national institutions such as government, political parties, police and religious bodies, Busters have almost none . . . Yet Xers are not without hopes, dreams or visions. They are a generation yearning for a better world and utterly committed to depth and integrity in human relationships. It

is a generation more open to questions of meaning and
spirituality than any other in the West over the past 200
years . . . (Starkey, 1997, pp. 28–9)

Starkey therefore sees 'Generation X' as responding to the trau-
matic circumstances in which they have lived by, in part, rejecting
values of the 'boomer' generation that preceded them. Whilst
this rejection could be seen in negative terms, Starkey identifies
positive elements within it such as a preference for community
over individualism and personal ambition, and a critical
approach to ideas and social institutions. Within this quote from
Starkey, as well, there is a sense of 'Generation X' as a generation
that both deeply desires meaning in life but is sceptical about
finding it in traditional ideas or institutions. Facing this dilemma,
it has been argued that 'Generation X' has turned to popular
culture as its primary source of meaning. Tom Beaudoin (1998),
for example, has suggested, that left to amuse themselves as
they grew up, 'Generation X' children immersed themselves in
various forms of popular culture, in particular TV, film, popular
music and video games. We will return to Beaudoin's idea that
popular culture functions as the 'surrogate clergy' of 'Generation
X' later in this book, but for now it is helpful simply to note his
claim that:

> During our lifetimes, especially during the critical period of
> the 1980s, pop culture was the amniotic fluid that sustained
> us. For a generation of kids who had a fragmented or com-
> pletely broken relationship to 'formal' or 'institutional'
> religion, pop culture filled the spiritual gaps . . . Pop culture
> provides the matrix that contains much of what counts as
> 'meaning' for our generation. As Douglas Rushkoff pithily
> observes, Generation X has an uncanny 'ability to derive
> meaning from the random juxtaposition of TV commercials,
> candy wrappers, childhood memories, and breakfast treats.'
> (Beaudoin, 1998, pp. 21f.)

For some (usually younger) writers, then, 'Generation X' is a
generation of people who have faced a difficult emotional and
social environment climate as they grew up, but who, through
this adversity, have developed a resourceful and distinctive

approach to life. For other (often older) writers, however, 'Generation X' is viewed in more negative terms as a whining, apathetic and disengaged generation. In the book, *Generation X Goes to College*, Peter Sacks (1996) describes how he took a career change from journalism to work as a college professor. He paints a picture of his 'Generation X' students as being un-motivated, often discourteous, wanting to be entertained rather than taught and expecting high grades without necessarily putting in the work to achieve them. Eventually, Sacks claims that the only way he could work with these students was to treat them like nursery school children, by only setting work that was fun for them, praising them whatever their contributions to the group and consistently giving them higher grades than their work really merited. A similarly jaundiced view of 'Generation X' creeps through in the writing of P. J. O'Rourke:

> Coupland's first novel, *Generation X*, was a detailed account of how wretched and spitty life is for middle-class kids born after 1960. 'Our parents had more' is the title of Chapter 2. In case you missed the point (or fell asleep while the plot ossified) Coupland included several pages of depressing statistics at the back of *Generation X*, e.g. according to a *Time*/CNN telephone poll taken in June of 1990, 65% of 18–29 year-old Americans agree that 'given the way things are, it will be much harder for people in my generation to live as comfortably as previous generations.'
>
> Of course it's difficult for these youngsters to know if they're going to live as comfortably as their parents did because these kids are so immobilized by despair over eco-logical ruin, shrinking white-collar job market, and fear of intimacy that they're all still living at home. (O'Rourke, 1994, p. 6)

It is clear that 'Generation X' is a controversial term, with some writers choosing to see this group as one that has developed distinctive and highly valuable qualities in the midst of adversity, and others choosing to see it as a generation of slackers and whiners. In the midst of these differences there is a broad con-sensus that 'Generation X' is a generation of people who share a particular 'peer personality' (Howe and Strauss, 1993). This 'peer personality' is generally seen as comprising the following qualities:

- members of 'Generation X' are disengaged from traditional sources of meaning and suspicious of traditional sources of authority;
- 'Generation X' is a generation whose prospects (for the first time in many generations) appear worse than that of their parents' generation, yet who do not necessarily equate well-being with material prosperity;
- 'Generation X' has been traumatised by social and relational instability;
- 'Generation X' lacks a sense of meaning, but also has a significant interest in the pursuit of meaning;
- 'Generation X' defines itself primarily in relation to popular culture.

If there is such a specific generational group as 'Generation X' that shares these qualities, then this clearly has implications for the Christian Church. Given falling numbers of particularly its younger members, we can see why it might be important for the Church to think seriously about how members of 'Generation X' can be constructively involved in its life and work. At the same time, however, the suspicion that is often noted amongst 'Generation X' towards traditional ideas and institutions that have failed to deliver a better world, suggests that Christian orthodoxy would need to adapt itself or present itself in new ways to be credible to this group. In the light of this, it is perhaps unsurprising that there is now a growing literature on how the Church might 'connect' with 'Generation X' in a way that still preserves important elements of orthodox Christian belief and practice (see, e.g., Mahedy and Bernadi, 1994; Bonacci, 1996; Starkey, 1997; Schieber and Olsen, 1999). Despite this growing literature on how to make religious connections with 'Generation X', there are good grounds for being suspicious of the idea of 'Generation X' that actually underpins it, and it is to these suspicions that we will now turn.

Moving beyond 'Generalization X'

So far in this chapter we have noted a range of books that make quite confident claims about 'Generation X'. Under closer scrutiny, however, we may wish to question quite how sound some of these claims actually are. We can begin, for example, with the issue of the years that mark the beginning and end of the period when 'Generation X' were born. In her book on *Marketing to Generation X*, Karen Ritchie (1995) explains that it is 'instinctively more satisfying' to see 1961 as the first year in which members of 'Generation X' were born (p. 16). In other words, it is preferable to use dates like 1961 or 1981 because they look neater. This may give rise to suspicions that clear definitions of between which years members of 'Generation X' were born are actually rather arbitrary. This would certainly help to explain why different writers actually give quite different dates. Thus whilst Howe and Strauss (1993) see 1961 as the first birth year for members of 'Generation X', Reifschneider (1999) states this is 1964 (p. 19), and both Barna and Dunn suggest it is 1965 (see Beaudoin, 1998, p. 28). An even wider span of years is given for the last birth year for 'Generation X'. Dunn states this is 1976, Howe and Strauss and Reifschneider claim it is 1981, and Barna proposes 1983.

Given that there is no clear agreement on which years mark the beginning and end of 'Generation X' births, we might want to question why writers continue to insist on using specific dates when they are talking about 'Generation X'. A sympathetic response to this literature could be that there are indeed correct dates that could be given for this generation and that some of these writers have got it right and the rest have got it wrong. In the absence of any clear criteria on how to judge which years are right and wrong, however, we may begin to suspect that using specific dates is, in fact, a rhetorical strategy for making it seem more plausible that a specific generational cohort called 'Generation X' actually exists.

Our doubts about some of the literature about 'Generation X' may deepen if we consider one or two of the specific claims made about this group in more detail. Peter Brierley (2000), for example, reports a summary of 'Generation X' traits which includes statements such as 'they have an insatiable appetite for junk food, junk films, junk ideas and junk culture' and 'they would rather be at a U2 concert than in church singing hymns' (pp. 104–6). If we give these more than a moment's thought, it is evident that they are fairly bland stereotypes. It might not, for example, take you very long to identify someone you know who falls within the 'Generation X years', who is not insatiably hooked on junk culture. Similarly, whilst it is almost certainly true that most people aged between twenty and forty in Britain today would rather be at a U2 concert than singing hymns, this claim conceals the fact that there are things that many such people would also do in preference to being at a U2 concert. When one notes the idea, that occurs not infrequently in this literature, that the band REM are important spokespersons for this whole generation (see, e.g., Beaudoin, 1998; Cox, 1998), then the sense deepens that at least some of the claims being made here are stretched too far to be credible. Any scepticism that we might feel towards some of these claims finds further support from sociological research that suggests that members of 'Generation X' do not demonstrate widely different social attitudes to their elders. Thus, for example, Wade Clark Roof's extensive research amongst Americans of the 'baby-boomer' generation (1999) suggests that 'baby-boomers' are just as likely to be critical of institutions and engaged in a personal pursuit of meaning as their 'baby-buster' offspring.

One commentator has observed that rather than talking about 'Generation X', it is in fact more accurate to talk about *'Generalization X'* because the concept of 'Generation X' has become a vehicle for loading a range of stereotypes onto a group of people born between a particular set of years (alt.culture, 2001). What is perhaps remarkable is that some of the writers who describe the qualities of 'Generation X' as a specific generational group show an awareness of the dangers of making broad generalizations about this group, and then fall into the trap of doing precisely that. So what is it about the idea of a generalized 'Generation X' that is attractive to so many writers?

It is possible to identify two separate agendas that underlie the use of the term 'Generation X' to denote a specific generational group. Firstly, it is evident that a range of writers are using the term as a focus for an 'inter-generational' dispute that has emerged between older and younger people in contemporary Western society, particularly in the United States. This point is quite evident in the tone in which we saw 'Generation X' described earlier in this chapter. For example, Geoffrey Holtz is using the concept of 'Generation X' as a platform for his argument that younger Americans have experienced neglect from their elders. By contrast, writers like Sacks and O'Rourke are using the concept as a means of highlighting that younger people are apathetic, lazy whingers who have unrealistically high expectations of life compared to the amount of effort that they are prepared to put into it. The fact that Kristoffer Cox's book *GenX and God* (1998) explicitly seeks to promote inter-generational understanding is a further indication of the generational argument that sometimes underlies the use of the term 'Generation X'. Whether there is anything particularly distinctive about this argument between older and younger Americans – or whether it is simply another example of the tensions that can emerge between youth culture and the wider culture of a society (Pilcher, 1995, pp. 134ff.) – is a question that goes beyond the scope of our discussion here. At this point, though, it is simply worth noting that for some writers the concept of 'Generation X' seems to function as a means to an end for making points either about the victimization or lack of virtue amongst younger people.

A second agenda also influences a great deal of the use of the term 'Generation X', and this latter agenda has a more immediate influence on much of the literature that talks about 'Generation X' in a religious context. A clue about the nature of this agenda is given when Christine Reifschneider (1999) tries to justify making broad generalizations about 'Generation X' by saying: 'What is the value of generalizing about a generation? . . . Knowing these general characteristics, even when they don't apply . . . to every Gen Xer you know, can give you a foundation for understanding and more effectively connecting with Generation X' (p. 19). What Reifschneider is saying here, then, is that even if the idea of a 'Generation X' with certain attitudes and traits does not hold true in the case of every young adult, such a concept is still a helpful tool for engaging with a particular group in contemporary society. Reifschneider's view of the term 'Generation X' is reflected amongst a number of other authors. Indeed, it is striking that the areas in which people have been most keen to write about 'Generation X' include marketing, religion and management. Underlying this range of literature is the assumption that if we understand the attitudes and traits of 'Generation X' then we can act towards young adults in more productive ways – whether our intention is to sell them a particular product, evangelise them or manage them more effectively.

It was precisely this belief that the term 'Generation X' could help organisations to target young adults more effectively that led to an explosion of interest in the term in the early 1990s. Douglas Coupland, writing about the aftermath of the publication of his novel *Generation X*, has commented:

> The problems started when trendmeisters everywhere began isolating small elements of my characters' lives – their offhand way of handling problems or their questioning of the status quo – and blew them up to represent an entire generation . . . Then the marketing began . . . Around this time my phone started ringing with corporations offering from $10,000 and up to talk on the subject of "How to Sell to Generation X". I said no. (The Gap asked me to do an ad. It was tempting, but I politely refused). In late 1991, after both political parties had called to purchase advice on X, I basically withdrew from the whole tinny discourse. (Coupland, 1995, p. 72)

There are particular reasons why the idea of 'Generation X' became so fascinating for those involved in marketing in the early 1990s (see Klein, 2001, pp. 67ff.). In the 1980s, in the United States, major companies selling products to individual consumers had been focusing their brands on 'baby-boomers' who were perceived as the most commercially lucrative market. By the early 1990s, however, people in the 'baby-boomer' age range were starting to buy cheaper, non-branded goods (such as supermarket 'own-brand' products) in preference to the products of the leading brand names. This shift generated considerable anxiety amongst large companies who started to see both their profits and share prices fall. The emerging idea of a 'Generation X' therefore greatly interested people involved in marketing for these businesses as it seemed to offer an alternative, younger market at which advertising could be targeted and to which products could be sold.

The marketing world thus became interested in the idea of 'Generation X' because major businesses were losing market share and were desperate to find a new group to sell their products to. A similar process can be seen in the growing interest in the idea of 'Generation X' in religious circles. In the same way that major companies were losing market share in the early 1990s, so many churches in Britain and, to a certain extent, America found their congregations falling as the decade progressed (see Gibbs, 2000). The fact that declining church membership was particularly acute amongst younger adults meant that an idea such as 'Generation X', which seemed to promise an insight into what it would mean to devise more user-friendly services or appropriate evangelism for young people, inevitably had its attraction. As a concept, 'Generation X' again became a means to an end, whether that end be increasing sales or increasing adherence to the Christian faith.

To summarise, then, much of what is written about 'Generation X' seems to be a set of broad and, quite often, unsustainable generalizations about a group of people born between a particular set of years. As we have seen here, the term 'Generation X' has been taken up by people who either want to make points in ongoing arguments about the relative merits or failings of young people, or who want a concept which they believe will help them to target younger adults more effectively with their products, beliefs or practices. If we are uninterested in getting into an 'inter-generational' slanging match, and do not have a particular product, belief-system or organisation that we wish to market to young people, then we may begin to wonder if the concept of 'Generation X' has anything to offer us at all. Indeed, like Douglas Coupland, we may feel that the concept is now so loaded with 'inter-generational' and marketing agendas that it is better simply to abandon it.

In this book, however, I want to suggest that attending to the idea of 'Generation X' is one very helpful way of understanding what is going on with religion, and with the wider search for meaning, in contemporary culture. To use the concept of 'Generation X' effectively, however, I want to suggest that we need to think about it not as a way of defining a particular generational group, but rather, as Douglas Coupland has put it, as 'a term that defines not a chronological age but a way of looking at the world' (1995, p. 72). So if 'Generation X' is not a literal generation of young adults but a way of approaching or understanding life, what is this 'Generation X' attitude and why has it developed in contemporary culture? We will explore the answers to these questions in the final part of this chapter.

Will the real 'Generation X' please stand up?

To understand more effectively the nature of a 'Generation X' view of the world, I believe we need to think closely about major social processes that have taken place within Western culture. A common reading of Western history over the past four centuries is that Western culture has undergone a process of modernization in which there has been a shift away from a reliance on religious institutions towards institutions based on secular rationality. This period of Western culture is generally referred to as 'modernity', and writers have described this process of moving from a society based on religious beliefs and institutions towards a free market economy based on secular institutions as the 'project of modernity'.

Now it is clear that to move from a culture in which the Church and its doctrines had a central role in social organisation to a culture in which business and wider social life can be conducted without any reference to religion is a seismic shift. In describing this process, it is helpful to use the sociologist Zygmunt Bauman's metaphor of the project of modernity being a 'liquifying' process (2001). Thus, as modernity unfolded, a range of religious and social certainties began to dissolve and become more fluid. The pre-modern idea that one's social status (or one's 'estate') was entirely defined by one's parentage shifted to the idea of social status as 'class', in which 'class' has become more defined by one's education and occupation and in which movement between classes became more possible. Similarly the notion of there being one 'true' faith or Church to which full members of society should adhere dissolved into the notion that one's religious affiliation was a matter of personal choice and had no significant bearing on one's social standing. Modernity thus 'loosened up' traditional pre-modern attitudes and patterns of social organisation in ways that allowed new social institutions to emerge, including, in particular, large-scale businesses that could be run in rational and profitable ways.

It is widely argued now that the 'project of modernity' has run its course or is entering a new phase of its development. Social theorists have therefore variously described us as living now in a period of 'high', 'late' or 'post' modernity. Bauman himself argues that, although modernity has been a process of dissolving the social structures and religious ideas of pre-modern society, modernity has now reached a point of leaving us with its own certainties. The foremost certainty of modernity, in Bauman's view, is that of capitalism and the global free market economy as the primary basis of social organisation. This view is shared by other writers, and has even led to the suggestion that the collapse of communism in Eastern Europe represents the 'end of history' as it is difficult to envisage any long-term future for a social system other than capitalism (Sim, 1999).

Social organisation in contemporary society is certainly strongly based on commercial transactions. The main sites in which people meet in urban areas are now the 'cathedrals of consumption' such as shopping centres or entertainment parks (Ritzer, 1999). The expansion of commercial activity onto the Internet now also means that buying and selling goods is an activity that extends into people's homes. Furthermore, any element of popular culture in which large numbers of people are interested now finds itself quickly bound up with corporate interests that try to use these cultural activities as a way of generating revenue. Recent examples of this has been the relationship between football and the profitability of British cable TV companies such as BSkyB (Conn, 1997), the marketing of club culture through big brand names such as Cream and the Ministry of Sound (Collin, 1997), and the close relationship between New Age thinking and imprints of major international publishers.

Although the project of modernity may have resulted in the certainties of a society organised on the basis of a free market economy, it has also been argued that the development of modernity has left considerable uncertainties in its wake as well. In the last chapter, we noted Steve Bruce's idea that religious beliefs were being displaced in a society increasingly guided by a modern, scientific rationality. Major social institutions do indeed continue to plan and structure their work on a modern, rational basis (with 'McDonald's' restaurants being an excellent example of this, see Ritzer, 2000). It can also be argued, however, that within contemporary Western society more generally there is a growing scepticism about the ability of such rational planning and thinking to address major problems of our time. The German social theorist Ulrich Beck (1992) has, for example, argued that we now live in a 'risk society' in which we are increasingly aware of the damaging social and environmental consequences of modern, industrial society. At the same time, however, Beck suggests that we are increasingly aware that these problems are too complex to be solved by a clear, rational plan (whether scientific, political or economic) devised by experts. In his view, this means that there are no longer 'big' rational theories or solutions that seem convincing to us, and that 'living and acting in uncertainty becomes a kind of basic experience' in contemporary culture (Beck *et al.*, 1994, p. 12).

Beck's notion of uncertainty as being the basic experience of contemporary life connects with an idea held by Bauman about the liquifying effects of modernity on our individual lives. Bauman argues that as modernity has solidified around social structures based on capitalism and the global free market, so the liquifying effects of modernity are now felt more powerfully at the level of individuals' sense of identity and meaning. In other words, we now find ourselves much less sure about how to live our lives. Partly this uncertainty reflects the fact that we are far more exposed – both through our personal experience and through the media – to different ideas about what it means to live well or to express ourselves as human beings (Gergen, 1991). TV programmes and magazines present us with an array of stories of different lifestyle choices that people make in terms of the work they do, the way they spend their leisure time, the relationships they conduct or the manner in which they express their sexuality. In the face of these different stories of how people live their lives, it becomes a matter of choice for each individual as to what kind of identity they want to build for themselves and what kind of life they want to lead. Clearly this is not a matter of completely free choice – our life-experiences and our gender, ethnicity and social class may often influence what kinds of choices we can make.[2] Nevertheless, living as an individual in contemporary culture has become what Anthony Giddens (1991, p. 5) has called a 'reflexive project' – a conscious process of making choices about how we define ourselves and act in the world.[3]

I want to argue here that a 'Generation X' view of the world is in fact a particular attitude towards this process of making sense of who we are and how we should live in the contemporary world. Indeed Douglas Coupland's novel *Generation X* can be understood as an attempt to address precisely this issue. Describing this book, Coupland writes:

> [*Generation X*] was about three strangers who decided to pull back from society and move to the fringe of Palm Springs, California, where they worked at dreary jobs at the bottom of the food chain. Together, they spent time trying to relocate their individual identities inside a new psychic landscape where personal memory fights for real estate with commercial memories. As they searched for meaning, all three sensed that their withdrawal was an act of sanity rather than negation; their worldview was simultaneously ironic and sentimental, and it reflected a way of thinking that I had never before seen documented. (Coupland, 1995, p. 72)

The characters in this novel (and in Coupland's work more generally) can therefore be understood as engaged in exactly the kind of conscious search for personal meaning that Baumann and Giddens are writing about. What is distinctive about their search, however, is their difficulty in finding meaning either in traditional ideas or in lifestyles presented through advertising or consumer culture more generally. Traditional structures such as family or religion have (at best) ambiguous meanings for Coupland's characters, and these cannot be uncritically embraced as the source of meaning to life. Defining oneself through the images and products provided within consumer culture is equally uncompelling, for it takes a special kind of self-deception to convince oneself that the meaning of one's life can be found in something that has been obviously created and marketed as a source of revenue for corporate interests. A 'Generation X' attitude is thus one of 'incredulity towards metanarratives' (see Lyotard, 1984), in which grand theories or stories of the world, whether economic, psychological, social, political or religious, no longer seem compelling or convincing. From a 'Generation X' perspective it is all too easy to see the flaws and limitations of these theories, and to see a wholehearted acceptance of them as unattractively naïve. Indeed, for those with a 'Generation X' view of the world, meaning is not something that can be found in pre-packaged forms in churches, shops or political parties, but rather meaning (if it is found at all) has to be sought in a personal way.

In summary, then, I want to suggest here that a 'Generation X' view of the world is a product of Western culture in which capitalism and the free market have emerged as fixed points of social organisation whilst personal meaning is fluid and unclear. A 'Generation X' view of the world, reflecting the themes of Coupland's fiction, is therefore one in which there is a profound sense both of the need for meaning and of the difficulty of finding ultimate meaning within contemporary culture. The 'Generation X' search for meaning is a personal one, in which there is a basic scepticism to the received or pre-packaged truths of churches, political parties or commercial organisations. The failure to establish meaning in one's life (or the failure of one's frameworks of meaning to live up to expectations) can lead to disappointment and despair, and an ironic approach to life can serve as a substitute for the search for deeper sources of meaning. But at the heart of the 'Generation X' perspective lies the aware-ness that the pursuit of personal meaning remains a key part of contemporary existence.

The definition of the 'Generation X' view of the world that I am presenting here clearly has some affinities to definitions of 'Generation X' attitudes that we noted at the beginning of this chapter. In particular, the emphases that we noted in the quote from Mike Starkey, that 'Generation X' is associated with a desire for meaning and a scepticism towards traditional institutions and ideas, both arise in the definition that I am offering. A significant difference between them, however, is that I think it is a mistake to associate 'Generation X' qualities with any particular age-group. Rather I believe it is important that the term 'Generation X' is primarily understood as a particular *attitude* that emerges in a 'late' or 'post' modern culture in which capitalism provides the fixed foundation of social organisation whilst the meaning of life on a personal level is in flux. At this stage, the distinction between seeing 'Generation X' as an actual generation of people or as a way of looking at the world may seem relatively trivial. In actual fact, though, I believe the way in which we define 'Generation X' will have a significant bearing on our interpretation of trends in the contemporary search for meaning. If we see 'Generation X' primarily as a generation of young adults, then we will try (as many people do) to emphasise similarities between different kinds of religious and non-religious activities that young adults engage in. If we do this, though, I think we will miss the very important point that the search for meaning in contemporary culture is not shaped primarily along *generational* lines, but by fundamentally different *attitudes* that people have towards the nature of truth, the role of external authorities and the significance of personal authenticity.

In this chapter, then, we have looked at different ways in which the term 'Generation X' has been understood, and I have presented what I believe to be a more adequate understanding of the term. In the remainder of this book we will now turn our attention to the implications of this 'Generation X' attitude both for religion and for individuals' search for meaning in contemporary culture more generally.

3
Flat-pack Furniture and Meccano Sets: 'Generation X' and Evangelical Christianity

At the beginning of chapter 1, I mentioned how I had changed from being a committed Evangelical Christian to someone who would no longer regard himself as having a mainstream Christian faith. Far from being unique in this shift, I can see how many of my peers from college days have changed along similar lines. Indeed I very much doubt that today's membership of the Durham University Christian Union would be that impressed by the current beliefs and lifestyles of many of us who were members of it some fifteen years ago.

Over the past few years, though, I have become aware of a wider trend within the Evangelical Christianity that I grew up in. Some people, like me, are moving away from it to the point where they would no longer regard themselves as Christians at all. Others have adopted a more open approach to their faith and are trying out ideas from other parts of the Christian tradition that might previously have been regarded with suspicion as being theologically 'unsound'. Whilst mainstream Evangelicalism (something we shall define below) remains an active and growing movement, there is also a gradually increasing number of people who are moving away from core Evangelical beliefs and assumptions. In this chapter, I want to explore how for some people this movement away from traditional Evangelical beliefs and practices represents an expression of the 'Generation X' search for meaning that we began to think about in the last chapter. Before doing this, however, it will be useful first to think about the core characteristics of mainstream Evangelical Christianity.

Who are the Evangelicals?

Evangelicalism is a particular form of Protestantism that has emerged since the Reformation. John Stott, one of the leading figures in contemporary Evangelicalism in Britain, has defined Evangelical Christians as 'Bible people' and 'gospel people' (Tidball, 1994, pp. 11–18; see also Bebbington, 1989, pp. 1–19; Saward, 1987). Evangelicals are 'Bible people' in the sense that they understand the text of the Bible to be the authoritative word of God, and believe that matters of faith, doctrine and ethics should ultimately be guided by reference to scriptural truth. Whilst there is some degree of disagreement amongst Evangelicals on doctrinal or moral issues, there tends to be a consensus within Evangelicalism that the Bible contains a core message which demands a human response – this is the sense in which Evangelicals are 'gospel people'. This core biblical message focuses on the crucifixion of Christ, which Evangelicals understand as an act of atonement for human sin which enables individuals to have a new relationship with God. To receive the benefit of Christ's atoning self-sacrifice, it is necessary for each individual to make a personal response of accepting God's forgiveness of them and to commit themselves to living a new life with God. This strong Evangelical emphasis on conversion leads to the popular labelling of Evangelicals as 'born-again' Christians. Following a personal experience of conversion, Evangelicals believe it is important for the individual to continue to lead a committed Christian life – a commitment which is often referred to as 'discipleship'. This commitment can find expression in social activism, a commitment to take part regularly in religious services, and a willingness to engage in regular acts of devotion through personal prayer and study of the Bible. Finally the Evangelical commitment to this core 'gospel' message is such that Evangelicals place an important emphasis on evangelism, the process of bringing this 'good news' to others who have not made a personal Christian commitment in the hope that they too will undergo an experience of conversion.

Evangelical theology therefore typically involves an emphasis on the authority of the Bible as the word of God, the central importance of Christ's redeeming self-sacrifice on the cross, the need to make a personal response to God's offer of forgiveness, to lead a committed Christian life and to bring the good news of the Christian faith to others. In addition to this distinctive theology, Evangelical Christianity also functions as a distinctive sub-culture (Tomlinson, 1995, pp. 6f.; Ward, 1996). There are Evangelical books and magazines, Evangelical pop music, Evangelical radio and TV stations, and major Evangelical events and conferences such as the Spring Harvest conference held over the Easter holiday. Even those people who write and record Evangelical worship songs find themselves occupying a celebrity status in Evangelical circles (Bullivant, 2001). This Evangelical sub-culture also tends to be clearly defined by certain conventions of individual behaviour, such as a disapproval of smoking or any other recreational drug use beyond moderate drinking, a negative attitude towards sexual behaviour outside of the context of heterosexual marriage, and a general refrain from gambling or swearing. The persistence of these traditional values in contemporary Evangelicalism is demonstrated by the response recently given on an 'agony' page on an Evangelical website to a teenage girl who had asked whether her church youth-leader was right to say that she should not go clubbing:

> Firstly, try not to be too mad at your youth leader, he is just looking out for you. His concern is probably because clubs are a great source of temptation in terms of drugs, alcohol and sex, stuff that can end up trashing your life. Clubbing can be great fun but I think you need to be aware of the environment that you are in. You say that you are not going too far with blokes but whose standards are you going by, yours or God's? And also are you putting yourself in a situation where you might be tempted to go further? (Soul Survivor, 2001)

Whilst to some outsiders these Evangelical standards may appear to be an expression of traditional (pre-1960s) middle-class values, within Evangelicalism itself they are generally understood to be an integral part of living obediently to God's will as revealed in the Bible. Similarly the drive to produce Evangelical books, magazines and CDs can reflect an Evangelical concern that the media in contemporary society often falls short of the standards of Christian truth and morality. Evangelical theology and the Evangelical sub-culture are thus closely bound together.

In several respects the Evangelical view of the world seems to be the antithesis of the 'Generation X' attitude as we have defined it here. Whereas 'Generation X' individuals can be profoundly conscious of the difficulty in establishing personal meaning, Evangelical Christians typically see the truth about existence as being clearly accessible through the words of Scripture. Furthermore, whilst a 'Generation X' attitude entails a scepticism towards 'pre-packaged' truth based on some kind of external authority, Evangelical Christians place a strong value on the communication of biblical 'truths' by respected preachers and writers within the Evangelical movement (Guest, 2002). Evangelical Christians are not immune from the pressures of our 'late' or 'post' modern culture, however, and the experience of living within a context of cultural diversity and uncertainty has lead some Evangelicals to question a number of assumptions within Evangelicalism. Such individuals may find themselves identifying strongly with a 'Generation X' view of the world, whilst at the same time being profoundly conscious that a Christian commitment is an important part of their lives. With the evident tension between traditional Evangelical and 'Generation X' attitudes, it is unsurprising that individuals who are Evangelical Christians but who also sympathise with a 'Generation X' view of the world have struggled to find forms of Christian identity and community that fit with their understanding of themselves and the world. In the remainder of this chapter, we will look at some of the forms that 'Generation X' Christianity is taking as it emerges out of the Evangelical movement.

The post-evangelical

Since its publication in 1995, Dave Tomlinson's book *The Post-Evangelical* has become a key text for individuals who are struggling to reconcile their Evangelical background and 'Generation X' sympathies. Originally raised in a Brethren church, Tomlinson become heavily involved in the Charismatic Renewal Movement as it developed in Britain in the 1970s and by the 1980s he was the leader of a network of new Charismatic Evangelical churches (see Walker, 1998, pp. 343–56). Increasingly, however, Tomlinson became disillusioned with what he perceived to be the rigid and authoritarian nature of the theology and practice of both his own network and the wider movement of which it was a part. He dissolved the network of churches that he was leading and became primarily involved in a project previously set up by that network called Holy Joe's. Holy Joe's began as an experiment in an alternative form of church, with meetings taking place in a pub in South London. The format of meetings would vary from informal Bible study discussions to worship sessions with a meditative feel to them, and the ethos of open enquiry went beyond what many members of Holy Joe's had previously experienced in Evangelical churches.

Tomlinson's experience of being at Holy Joe's made him increasingly aware of a group of people who, like him, had their roots in the Evangelical movement but who were more and more dissatisfied with the rigid ideas of Evangelical theology and ethics. His decision to write *The Post-Evangelical* was motivated largely by a pastoral concern that disillusioned Evangelicals were beginning to abandon their Christian faith and commitment altogether. Tomlinson comments on a letter he received from a man complaining that he had suffered twenty years of being told what to think and do in Evangelical circles – 'I've had enough of it', he wrote. 'It's time for me to make up my own mind' (p. 3). Tomlinson goes on to say that for people such as this who are profoundly disenchanted with the authoritarian nature of their Evangelical backgrounds, there is a desire for a more 'grown-up' church environment in which 'there were fewer predigested opinions and fewer categorical conclusions, and where there was a lot more space to explore alternative ideas' (p. 4). In writing *The Post-Evangelical*, then, Tomlinson hoped to offer an understanding of Christianity to which people from an Evangelical background could relate, which also took seriously their doubts and questions about their faith.

In this book, Tomlinson defines a post-evangelical as someone who accepts 'many of the assumptions of Evangelical faith, while at the same time moving beyond its perceived limitations' (p. 7). The post-evangelical is thus someone who still accepts basic tenets of Evangelical faith such as the existence of God as a reality beyond ourselves (p. 93), and the importance of the Bible as a source of inspiration for Christian life (pp. 104ff.). A post-evangelical is therefore someone who retains a basic Christian commitment. At the same time, however, Tomlinson argues that the 'post-modern' character of contemporary society leaves many people with an underlying sense of uncertainty and scepticism towards any attempt to explain the meaning of life with reference to any single 'grand narrative'. For people (including Evangelical Christians) living in this post-modern context, Tomlinson argued that it was therefore much harder to accept uncritically the clear and absolute truth claims made by Evangelical theology (see pp. 75ff.). He commented:

> The challenge to churches of all traditions is how to adjust to the changes which are taking place, and how to express eternal truth in and through this emerging culture. It seems to me that there is a basic separation from those who see the only solution to be that of returning (in some cases with a vengeance) to the older certainties; in effect these people are saying that the only response to a sea of uncertainty is to re-establish the presence of absolute certainty. This approach is understandable, and it is clear that there is a considerable 'market' for it. After all, it offers a sense of security and familiarity in the midst of a lot of confusion. But for lots of us, it just will not do. (pp. 139f.)

In other words, once the genie of uncertainty and critical scepticism towards 'pre-packaged' truth had been let out of the bottle within Western culture, it was no longer possible for many Christians to maintain a simple, unquestioning faith in Evangelical theology without doing considerable damage to their sense of integrity. Tomlinson thus argued that there was a need for a new understanding of Christian faith based on the Evangelical tradition that was relevant to the contemporary cultural climate of uncertainty, diversity and criticism of 'received' truth.

The kind of Christian identity and theology that Tomlinson advocated is compatible with a 'Generation X' view of the world. Rather than adopting the traditional Evangelical emphasis on upholding the clear, core truths of the gospel, Tomlinson argued for an approach to Christian faith that emphasised openness, exploration and personal authenticity (pp. 58ff.). This is demonstrated in a 'parable' that Tomlinson tells, following the style of Jesus' parable of the Pharisee and the Tax-Collector:

> 'A Spring Harvest (major Evangelical conference) speaker and a liberal bishop each sat down to read the Bible. The Spring Harvest speaker thanked God for the precious gift of the Holy Scriptures and pledged himself once again to proclaim them faithfully. "Thank you, God," he prayed, "that I am not like this poor bishop who doesn't believe in your word, and seems unable to make his mind up whether or not Christ rose from the dead." The bishop looked puzzled as he flicked through the pages of the Bible and said, "Virgin birth, water into wine, physical resurrection. I honestly don't know if I can believe these things, Lord. In fact, I'm not even sure that I believe you exist as a personal Being, but I am going to keep searching." I tell you that this liberal bishop rather than the other man went home justified before God. For everyone who thinks he has arrived at his destination has actually hardly begun, and he who continues searching is closer to his destination than he realizes.' (pp. 61f., see also p. 132)

Thus, rather than seeing absolute truth as something that is easily and immediately accessible from the pages of Scripture, or from Evangelical books or sermons, a post-evangelical perspective sees the pursuit of truth as an ongoing process of trying to establish personal meaning in response to the Christian tradition. There is a significant difference here then between the traditional Evangelical belief that truth is a single thing that can be easily identified on the basis of the external authority of the Bible, and the post-evangelical idea that truth is complex, never fully understood and needs to be grasped in ways that are personally authentic (p. 87). In describing these different perspectives on the notion of truth, Tomlinson has differentiated between an Evangelical 'flat-pack' view of truth and a post-evangelical 'meccano' notion of truth (pp. 82f.). In the first of these views, truth is like a 'flat-pack' piece of furniture in which the pieces can only be fitted together in one way to make a specific object. To see truth as more akin to a Meccano set, however, suggests that truth can take a number of different forms in the same way that the pieces of a Meccano set can be put together in a wide (though not endless) variety of forms. A distinction is therefore evident between a traditional Evangelical emphasis on the clear, literal truth of the Bible and the post-evangelical desire to adopt a more poetic and symbolic view of truth, in which the Christian faith can sustain a range of different interpretations and responses (pp. 114, 119).

Religious truth, for the post-evangelical, therefore emerges out of interaction between the Christian tradition and the personal perceptions, thoughts and values of the individual believer (p. 2). The significance of personal authenticity in this post-evangelical search for meaning should not be under-emphasised. Indeed the post-evangelical emphasis on pursuing meaning in a way that is true to oneself is illustrated in a striking way in the following vignette from a Holy Joe's meeting:

> [In a discussion at Holy Joe's] one man was brave enough to admit that he wanted a more conformist experience of Christianity and that he struggled when faced with too much uncertainty and ambiguity. Thankfully, the group resisted any temptation to argue him into a different position, and simply reassured him that his feelings were perfectly valid. (p. 50)

This story is interesting in that it suggests that, for a post-evangelical community such as Holy Joe's, personal authenticity in one's religious life is more important than any abstract theological principle. Thus, whilst post-evangelicals might want to hold a more open and complex view of Christian faith than the man in this story, it is significant that the group encouraged him to pursue a path that was personally authentic for him rather than trying to 'convert' him to a post-evangelical perspective. It is important to note, however, that for Tomlinson at least this emphasis on personal authenticity cannot be used to justify any kind of personal belief or action. Whilst post-evangelicals might place personal authenticity in high regard, their spirituality is still different to that of the 'self-spirituality' that Paul Heelas has identified within the contemporary New Age movement. New Age 'self-spirituality' rests on the assumption that truth is ultimately what is found to be true within oneself. This is subtly, though significantly different to the post-evangelical view that there is a God beyond us who is the source of truth and towards whom we must find personally authentic ways of relating.

This emphasis on an open, critical and personally authentic engagement with Christian faith makes it difficult to make any generalizations about what post-evangelicals *do* believe or what kind of ethical positions they are likely to take. Indeed some people whom I have met who would describe themselves as post-evangelical are clearer about what they do not believe than what they do believe. For some post-evangelicals, the more open nature of their search for meaning leads them to engage with other theological traditions and ideas (e.g. Celtic Christianity, Christian mysticism, creation spiritualities) that might not be seen as consistent with biblical truth in conventional Evangelical circles. Post-evangelicals often hold different, and usually more liberal ethical views than conventional Evangelicals, and one area in which this finds expression is in relation to sexual ethics. Thus, whereas Evangelicals have traditionally seen homosexual sexual acts as morally wrong, Tomlinson has, for example, publicly supported the validity of committed gay sexual relationships.

Despite the ambiguities surrounding post-evangelicalism, it seems reasonable to claim that the emerging 'post-evangelical' Christian identity represents an attempt by individuals and groups to retain a meaningful connection with the Christian faith in a way that reflects a 'Generation X' view of the world. The post-evangelical rejection of simple, unitary definitions of truth based on the external authority of the Bible reflects the 'Generation X' suspicion towards 'pre-packaged' and marketed versions of truth. Similarly the post-evangelical emphasis on an open, ongoing, personal pursuit of meaning reflects the 'Generation X' struggle to establish personal meaning in a cultural context of uncertainty and diversity. Where post-evangelicalism differs most clearly from a 'Generation X' view of the world (in the sense intended by Douglas Coupland) is in its fundamental commitment to the truth of the Christian tradition. Although post-evangelicals may be prepared to be more open and exploratory in their religious beliefs and practice, they do retain a belief in the existence of God and of the value of the Christian tradition. The characters in Coupland's novels would struggle to maintain this level of commitment to any one particular religious tradition as the primary source of meaning in life.

The concept of the 'post-evangelical' seems most significant at the moment as a way of offering a new kind of self-identity to Evangelical Christians who are feeling disillusioned by that tradition. At the same time, however, post-evangelical values are evident in a new approach to Christian worship that has largely emerged out of Evangelical churches. It is to this 'alternative worship' scene that we will now turn our attention.

'Alternative worship'

White paper leaves glowed starkly under the sole illumination of blacklight as we carried them to the beautifully sculpted wire tree and tied the ribbon to its branches. The Tree of Life bore our prayers as we knelt on one of seven cushions in a circle around a low white-gravel covered circular altar, incense drifting among us, electronic music carrying the mood. The priest intoned the words of the Great Thanksgiving, and we responded, 'Holy, Holy, Holy, the Lord God almighty, who was and is and is to come'. Bread and wine and a white stone were put into our hands. White clothing and papers glowed as they passed the blacklight. We reflected on our lives – explored or unexplored? Scripture was read. 'Unto the one who prevails I will give a white stone' (Revelation 2:17). A spoken meditation guided our private ones. We worshipped. We met with God. (Riddell *et al.*, 2000, p. 61)

This description of an 'alternative worship' service contains a number of features that are often present in such events. The event combined traditional elements of Christian liturgy (the Great Thanksgiving, the use of bread and wine) with unconventional religious images (the Tree of Life on which 'prayers' were tied, the giving of the white stone). Other elements of traditional (and non-evangelical) worship such as incense were used in conjunction with contemporary resources such as ambient, electronic music. Significant creative effort had gone into planning this event, and it is clear that for the person offering this description the service had a powerful aesthetic as well as spiritual element to it. It is also notable that this event was participatory – with people's prayers being tied to the Tree of Life – and an environment was created in which people could reflect and meditate upon their experience in the service.

If you have not attended a service of this kind, this description may even seem bizarre or it may be difficult to imagine such an event taking place in the context of Christian worship. Certainly some explanation needs to be given of how 'alternative worship' has come to develop, and of the ethos that typically informs alternative worship events.

If the concept of the 'post-evangelical' can be seen as a reaction against rigid, traditional Evangelical ideas of theological truth, then it may be possible to see alternative worship as a reaction to mainstream forms of Evangelical worship. Most groups who are experimenting with alternative forms of worship have their origins in (and are still associated with) Evangelical churches. Probably the best-known example of such a group was the Nine O'Clock Service, which was based within the Charismatic Evangelical church of St Thomas', Crooks in Sheffield. In the early to mid-1990s, the Nine O'Clock Service achieved a national reputation for its use of a range of multimedia technology (including contemporary ambient and dance music) in creating worship events which evoked more of an atmosphere of a nightclub than a church (Guest, 2002). Despite its public and controversial collapse in 1995, the Nine O'Clock Service served as an inspiration to many other groups to experiment in creating worship services that were imaginative and culturally relevant.

Since the 1980s mainstream Evangelical worship had itself experienced something of a renaissance, partly as a consequence of the writing of new worship songs and development of new worship styles inspired by the growing Charismatic movement. A new generation of Evangelical 'worship leaders' also began to emerge (of which probably the most well known was Graham Kendrick), and Evangelical conferences such as Spring Harvest became important opportunities not only for the dissemination of Evangelical teaching, but also for large-scale worship services led by these high profile figures. This tradition of high profile Evangelical worship leaders and large-scale worship events has continued since, with the Watford-based organisation Soul Survivor now offering an internationally recognised range of resources and events for mainstream Evangelical worship.

Whilst much Evangelical worship over this period began to adopt new forms – such as longer periods of singing which would lead into 'open' times of 'singing in tongues' and informal prayer – the ideology underlying the worship remained largely unchanged. One of the new generation of worship leaders in Britain recently commented that he was delighted when 'you hear some young worship leader and they have expressed an age-old biblical truth in a brand new way musically and lyrically' (Bullivant, 2001). This statement reflects the assumption within mainstream Evangelical worship that developments in worship consist of finding new ways of expressing core, traditional Evangelical ideas such as the primary importance of Christ's atoning sacrifice on the cross. New Evangelical churches (with a predominantly young adult membership) have also begun to emerge which adopt creative approaches to the setting and style of worship. One example, from the United States, is of a church called 'Mosaic' which meets in a nightclub, and uses a live band, multimedia presentations, art and dance within its services (Prieto, 2000). Whilst the style of worship clearly draws much from contemporary popular culture, it is clear that the ethos of Mosaic is still very much based in a traditional Evangelical ideology. The leadership of Mosaic strongly encourage 'bibli-cally-based' theology and ethics, and, for example, take a strongly negative view of gay sexual relationships or any form of sexual activity outside marriage (Prieto, 2000, pp. 68ff.). Thus whilst Evangelical worship may be taking more diverse forms (including forms which draw heavily on contemporary media), it is evident that underlying this worship a traditional Evangelical ideology is still very largely intact.[1]

As we saw in relation to the idea of the 'post-evangelical', however, some Evangelical Christians have become increasingly critical or disillusioned with the constraints of traditional Evangelical concepts and conventions. This has led not only to the post-evangelical revision of Evangelical theology but to the emergence of an alternative worship movement that seeks to move beyond church services constrained by traditional Evangelical ideology. One of the leading figures in this alternative worship movement, Mike Riddell, describes this process of disillusionment for himself in the following way:

> Increasingly I became aware of the great gulf separating the different streams of my life. It seemed that to enter a church building was to pass through into a different dimension, where everything was different and strange. In the ecclesial setting, none of the music I listen to was played, little of the language I spoke was used and none of the literature I read was mentioned. The sermons did not address any of the issues I struggled with or cared about. Nor was there any chance for me to discuss, to argue or to question. And yet that is the only way I know to process things for myself. As the initial romanticism of the Charismatic movement faded, I found myself moved to boredom and frustration by worship . . . I was bored . . . which is not good when you are the minister. (Riddell *et al.*, 2000, p. 9)

Individuals and groups within the alternative worship movement have therefore sought to develop new forms of church service which appeal to them more than mainstream Evangelical worship. Thus, whilst Evangelical worship often reflects the language and conventions of the Evangelical sub-culture, alternative worship events draw on language and resources from beyond that sub-culture whether that be in the form of a story from the *Big Issue* magazine, a contemporary piece of dance music or a visual image from a contemporary film. The use of these contemporary cultural resources is not understood within the alternative worship movement as an attempt to make Christian worship 'trendy' or appealing to others, but as an attempt to create environments for Christian worship that are culturally authentic for those who have planned the event. The website of one alternative service thus states that 'if we're using dance or pop music it is because it's part of our culture, if we're using multimedia it's because we're used to receiving and sending information in that format, if we're telling stories it's because that's how we share our thoughts and feelings in the pub and at work' (Host, 2001).

This emphasis on developing culturally authentic forms of worship is also connected to an emphasis within alternative worship on developing worship events that allow participants to engage in worship in diverse and personally authentic ways. In contrast to forms of mainstream Evangelical worship in which participants are encouraged to express specific attitudes (e.g. profound gratitude to God for his saving love), alternative worship events typically encourage participants to discover their own meaning in the event (see Guest, 2002). Alternative worship thus makes frequent use of traditional and contemporary symbols – candles, crosses, icons, sculpture or art/video installations – from which participants can draw their own meaning, rather than attempt to proscribe the meaning that participants draw from the worship through sermons or statements by worship leaders (Riddell *et al.*, 2000, pp. 62ff.).

The primary motivation for the design of alternative worship services can therefore be seen as the desire to develop an environment in which personally and culturally authentic experiences of God are possible (see Grace, 2001). Thus the organisers of the alternative service, Host, describe their primary aim in the following way:

> Host is our response to searching, exploring and expressing the spirituality of our lives. It is a continuing experiment fuelled by a desire to make sense of what we believe and how that affects our lives and the world in which we live.

It evolves as we continue to search for and discover the elements and environment in which to understand and respond to God with honesty, integrity and creativity. (Host, 2001)

A similar sentiment is expressed by the authors of *The Prodigal Project*, one of the leading books on the theory and practice of alternative worship:

We cannot hope to 'run a show' for others. We must seek to create a place that cuts into our own hearts and souls, where God can stir and soothe, rend and reunite us. If we can create something which is authentic for ourselves and the people with whom we stand, then perhaps others will identify with what we have begun to build, value the opportunity to make their own contribution and join us in our adventure. Around the fire the travellers gather; seeking realness, safety, honesty, integrity, openness, and tough love. (Riddell *et al.*, 2000, pp. 36f.)

The ethos of the alternative worship movement therefore contains a number of elements common to a 'Generation X' view of the world. There is an emphasis on the open-ended, creative and personally authentic search for meaning. Alternative worship services tend to be planned from scratch each time they take place rather than relying on the repetition of a particular liturgy, and this emphasises a notion of faith as a developmental process, 'a pilgrimage with no prescribed route or end' (Guest, 2002). Furthermore the suspicion towards meaning being dictated by some authoritative text or person leads to alternative worship groups typically functioning in democratic ways in the planning and leadership of services. As the Host (2001) website puts it, 'there is no priest or exclusive worship leader [for the group], instead members of the collective contribute elements to the worship: bible reading and ritual, art, prayer, meditation, music, activity, words and thoughts.' Another 'Generation X' trait which can be identified within the literature on alternative worship is a rejection of consumerism as a primary source of meaning and identity for individuals in Western culture. For example, Baker (2001a) comments that alternative worship is not only resistant to the dominant culture within Evangelical churches, but also resistant to the dominant culture of capitalism within Western society. As another writer puts it, alternative worship offers 'new exercises by which to engage and arouse the soul out of the torpor caused by consumerism' (Riddell *et al.*, 2000, p. 139).

As with the concept of the 'post-evangelical', then, the alternative worship scene can be understood as an attempt by people with an Evangelical background to create new religious identities and rituals that are congruent with a 'Generation X' view of the world. Does this mean, then, that post-evangelicalism and alternative worship are likely to become dominant forms of Protestant religion as we enter the twenty-first century? In the final part of this chapter, we will briefly explore what the implications may be of these 'Generation X' religious movements for the future of the Church in Britain.

The future's bright, the future's post-evangelical?

'Post-evangelicalism' and alternative worship can be seen, in a wider cultural sense, as an expression of the influence of 'late' or 'post' modernity on Evangelical Christianity. It would be a mistake, however, to assume that 'post-evangelicalism' or alternative worship are generally supplanting traditional forms of Evangelical theology or worship. Indeed mainstream Evangelicalism is one of the few branches of the Christian Church in Britain to have demonstrated any numerical growth in churches and members between 1989 and 1998 (Brierley, 2000). Within mainstream Evangelicalism, the theological emphasis on absolute truth discerned through God's Word in the Bible remains unchanged. One of the main tools for Evangelical church growth in recent years, the Alpha Course, has been described by one Evangelical as 'providing answers and certainty for people in moral direction, beliefs and lifestyle' (Shepherd, 2001). Mainstream Evangelicalism therefore appears to be continuing to flourish despite the obvious discontinuities in its ideology and practice with a 'Generation X' view of the world.

By contrast, the alternative worship movement in Britain is a relatively small and underground network. Similarly there are few self-consciously 'post-evangelical' churches, and many 'post-evangelicals' seem to exist in or around the fringes of mainstream Evangelical churches. It is also difficult to see significant growth taking place in the 'post-evangelical' or 'alternative worship' movements, precisely because of the reluctance within them to engage in activities aimed at 'converting' people to become new members. We noted in the earlier vignette from Holy Joe's that the group did not try to convert someone to a 'post-evangelical' perspective, but encouraged him to pursue a faith that was authentic to him, even if that took a more traditional Evangelical form. This emphasis on the personal pursuit of meaning, and a reluctance to try to impose religious beliefs or identities on individuals, is also evident in alternative worship groups. This point is illustrated in Guest's participant-observation research with an alternative worship group based at a large Evangelical church (2002). When Guest attended services at the main church, he found that members of the congregation were welcoming, but were also keen to establish whether or not he was a Christian and sought to 'convert' him when they discovered that he was not. By contrast, the members of the alternative worship service generally did not ask him about his religious identity and fully accepted him into the process of planning services as someone who was prepared to engage in an open search for meaning. This open, tolerant approach does have wider implications for the growth and publicity of the group, as Guest (2002) observes that ' . . . the fact that "alternative" worship resists any "pat" expressions of Christianity and repels from any "pushy", discursive forms of evangelism, has meant that it has no active mission strategy. Services are not heavily promoted, nor do organisers typically gauge their success by numerical factors' (p. 10). Alternative worship groups thus tend to evaluate the success of their services on the quality of religious experience that it made possible for participants, rather than the quantity of people who participated in the ritual. Whilst this emphasis is clearly congruent with alternative worship's concern for the pursuit of authentic personal meaning, and reflects a rejection of the more traditional Evangelical preoccupation with numerical church growth, it nevertheless has implications for the likely growth of the alternative worship network in the future.

Given that 'post-evangelicalism' and the 'alternative worship' movement are relatively small in relation to mainstream Evangelical Christianity, it may be tempting to dismiss these as peripheral phenomena within the contemporary Church. The fact that those who identify themselves as 'post-evangelicals' or who plan alternative worship services are mainly white, middle-class graduates, might also lead to the argument that these groups are only involving or engaging with a limited range of people within society. When the reluctance of 'post-evangelicals' and those involved in 'alternative worship' to convert others to their beliefs is acknowledged, it is clearly open to question as to how significant or influential 'post-evangelicalism' and 'alternative worship' will be in the development of Christianity in the coming decades.

To dismiss the notion of the 'post-evangelical' and the 'alternative worship' scene as peripheral to Christianity in Britain would, in my view, be a significant mistake. If we think about these 'Generation X' religious movements in the context of mainstream Evangelicalism then clearly the numbers of people involved in them are, and will most probably remain, smaller than those committed to traditional Evangelical beliefs and practices. If, however, we think about mainstream Evangelicalism in the context of religious observance in Britain as a whole, then it is evident that mainstream Evangelical Christianity is very much a minority form of religion which, in England, involves no more than 3 per cent of the total population (Brierley, 2000). In this chapter, I have argued that the 'post-evangelical' identity and the 'alternative worship' movements are an expression of 'Generation X' attitudes, which are themselves an expression of the cultural diversity and uncertainty of late modernity. If this is the case, then it may be that 'post-evangelicals' and 'alternative worship' are part of a much wider social trend towards the pursuit of personally authentic meaning and the rejection of rigid truth-claims based on some kind of external religious authority, whether that be God, the Bible or the Church. In this scenario, it is actually mainstream Evangelicalism that is peripheral to current trends in the contemporary search for meaning, with its continued adherence to a notion of absolute truth based on the authoritative word of God as revealed through the Bible. Thus, far from being peripheral phenomena, the 'post-evangelical' and 'alternative worship' could be understood as a Christian expression of a social trend towards the pursuit of personally meaningful and non-authoritarian beliefs, rituals and religious communities (Riddell *et al.*, 2000, p. 39), a broad trend which does also embrace the New Age movement (see Drane, 1991). The mainstream Evangelical movement may not be about to give up its core assumptions and warmly embrace 'post-evangelical' ideas and values; as Tomlinson observes, there is still an evident market for authoritarian forms of religion and the Evangelical movement will continue to draw on this in the coming decades. Nevertheless, the existence of the 'post-evangelical' Christian identity and the presence of alternative worship services does suggest that at least some parts of the Christian Church may be able to adapt in ways that will be accessible to people who share a 'Generation X' view of the world.

Whether the emergence of a 'Generation X' view of the world is indeed a significant social trend within Western culture is a question that merits further empirical research. It is clear from the low rate of church attendance, however, that if the 'Generation X' desire and struggle to find personal meaning is at all widespread, then much of this pursuit of personal meaning is now taking place outside of the context of organised religion. In the next two chapters we will turn our attention to what kinds of form this wider search for meaning in contemporary culture may be taking.

4

'MTV Is My Bible . . .'

> My most recent religious experience happened in the fourth
> row at the closing performance of the musical, *Rent* . . .
> During some songs people raised their hands in the air as
> if at an evangelical revival. They seemed to acknowledge
> that the drama – the liturgy – was *about* us and yet *beyond*
> us, giving meaning to our lives, and life to our fragmented
> existence. Still, I was astonished to hear a woman utter a
> quiet 'amen' after a song. (Tom Beaudoin, *Virtual Faith*)

Our discussion so far has raised some basic issues. From
statistical evidence of church attendance, it appears that formal
religious observance in Britain (certainly as concerns the
Christian Church) is in serious decline. The idea of a 'Generation
X' view of the world suggests, though, that individuals within
Western culture may still be interested in seeking meaning in life.
The way in which this desire for personally authentic meaning is
being expressed in (post)evangelical Christian circles was
explored in the previous chapter. It seems clear, however, that
for the majority of people in Western culture, any search for
meaning is not taking place through orthodox religious means.
We have already noted the declining membership of the Christian
Church. There has been significant growth in the numbers of
Buddhists, Muslims and Sikhs in Britain over the past decade,
but the combined number of people actively practising these
three religions still remains at less than 3 per cent of the total
British population (Brierley, 2000).[1] The proliferation of alternative spiritualities (in the forms of workshops, festivals and books)
suggests that a larger group of people in Britain may be pursuing
meaning through what can broadly be termed the 'New Age'

movement (Heelas, 1996), though it remains difficult to quantify exactly how culturally significant this movement really is.

If people within Western culture are still concerned with the pursuit of meaning, then what resources (if not orthodox religious ones) are helping them in their search? In this chapter and the following one, we shall explore the idea that popular culture[2] is an important medium and resource for the contemporary search for meaning for many individuals. Initially, in this chapter, we shall explore this idea by examining the work of a young American theologian, Tom Beaudoin, who has written about the 'religious' significance of popular culture. This will involve both understanding what Beaudoin has to say on this issue, as well as identifying some of the weaknesses in his ideas.

Beaudoin, 'Generation X' and 'Virtual Faith'

In his book *Virtual Faith*, Tom Beaudoin (1998) attempts to develop a theology 'by, for and about Generation X' (p. xiv). By this, Beaudoin means that he wants to try to understand the theological significance of 'Generation X' attitudes and experiences, to identify the theological beliefs of members of 'Generation X' and to stimulate theological discussion in a way that is helpful for members of 'Generation X'. These aims are important and ambitious, and Beaudoin himself recognises that this book is an early contribution to a discussion that needs much further development. There is not enough time for us here to consider in detail the whole of Beaudoin's argument in *Virtual Faith*, but we will turn our attention to one important strand of it that is particularly relevant to our own discussion here.

As we noted in chapter 2, Beaudoin is one of the writers who tends to see 'Generation X' as a particular generational cohort. Rather than trying to identify specific years between which members of 'Generation X' (or 'Xers') were born, however, Beaudoin is happier with a vaguer definition that sees 'Xers as those born between the early 1960s to the late 1970s' (p. 28). Indeed Beaudoin sees members of 'Generation X' as being defined not primarily by the particular year in which they were born, as by a particular attitude that they have towards popular culture.

According to Beaudoin, 'Generation X' and popular culture are inseparable. 'GenX cannot be understood apart from popular culture, and much of popular culture cannot be interpreted without attention to Generation X' (p. 22). Beaudoin believes that this close link between popular culture and 'Generation X' is a consequence of the experience of childhood and adolescence that many members of this generational group had. He repeats the claim that many 'Xers' grew up in families in which both parents were working, and that they turned to popular culture (in the form of TV, music and computer games) to amuse themselves in the times when they were free from school and parental super-vision. Alongside the investment of time and energy that these young 'Xers' put into popular culture, the forms and technologies of popular culture also underwent significant change from the late 1970s. With the growing use of the video recorder, home computer, games consoles, cable/satellite television and, more recently, the Internet, new forms of popular cultural activity and entertainment became available to this young social group. Popular culture therefore developed in new and exciting ways at precisely the point where a generation of children and teen-agers were becoming more dependent on mass-produced popular culture as a focus for their energies and as a way of learning about the world. Beaudoin thus goes as far as to describe popular culture as the 'amniotic fluid' within which members of 'Generation X' grew up.

In Beaudoin's view, then, popular culture represents an important frame of reference for members of 'Generation X'. Popular culture is thus important for 'Xers' as a shared pool of experiences and framework for conversation (as anyone who has spent time at a party in alcohol-fuelled discussions of *The Magic Roundabout* and *The Clangers* would concur). Beyond this, though, Beaudoin argues that popular culture has a religious significance for members of 'Generation X'. Indeed it is through popular culture that 'Xers' attempt to make sense of life and to express their deeper religious sentiments. Popular culture has thus become the 'surrogate clergy' (p. 21) for 'Generation X', offering a more immediate and accessible way of exploring issues of meaning than traditional, institutional religion. A fundamental assumption for Beaudoin here (and one to which we shall return in the next chapter) is that human beings inevitably have religious strivings as they attempt to make sense of their experience of living a finite and fragile existence. Following Paul Tillich, Beaudoin argues that this basic desire to seek and express fundamental meaning in life typically underlies all human culture (p. 30). For 'Generation X', the cultural form in which this search for, and expression of, meaning takes place is precisely the popular cultural forms of music videos, films and TV programmes, computer games and the Internet, as well as other leisure activities.

So far it is possible to see the basic pillars of Beaudoin's argument. 'Xers', like all human beings, have a need to search for and express fundamental ideas and beliefs about the meaning of life. Popular culture has a special significance in the lives of members of 'Generation X'. For 'Xers', the search for, and expression of, meaning thus primarily takes place through the medium of popular culture. Having built up this fundamental argument, though, what does Beaudoin have to say more specifically about the way in which popular culture represents a source of meaning for members of 'Generation X'?

Beaudoin develops this idea of the religious significance of popular culture by drawing an analogy between religious texts and the 'texts' of popular culture. In the same way that a formal religion will typically have certain texts that express something of that religion's view of existence, so Beaudoin argues that popular culture is made up of 'texts' that express particular views about the meaning of life. It is clear, though, that the 'texts' of popular culture that Beaudoin has in mind here go way beyond the written and printed word. He writes:

> By *text* I mean any popular culture 'event', from a dance to a bodily costume to a sporting event to a music video. I have considered three types of 'texts' in this book. In music video, the 'text' includes most fundamentally images and music, including lyrics. In cyberspace, the 'text' includes the medium of cyberspace, as well as many phenomena of virtual communication, including e-mail and sites in cyberspace. When it comes to costuming and bodily adornment,

> the 'text' includes many forms of 'fashion', including clothing and hairstyles. (p. 186)

The 'religious texts' of popular culture are not just written words then, but any kind of popular cultural activity that conveys some kind of meaning. Visual images in a pop video and the manner in which a person dresses can therefore express a view of the self and of the world just as much as a traditional printed text.

What Beaudoin is suggesting, then, is that popular culture offers a range of 'texts' that tell us something about the meaning of existence. Rather than having a core set of traditional religious Scriptures (although they may draw on these as well), members of 'Generation X' find meaning through music videos, CDs, films, websites and fashions. By analysing the popular cultural 'texts' that carry significance for members of 'Generation X', Beaudoin thus argues that it is possible to identify symbols, stories and ideas that are important in helping this group of people to make sense of life.

Beaudoin cites one such significant example of a 'Generation X' religious/popular cultural 'text' as the video to REM's song 'Losing My Religion' (p. 130). Within *Virtual Faith*, Beaudoin thus attempts a detailed analysis of what he takes to be the religious or theological meaning of this music video. He begins:

> The video for 'Losing My Religion' begins with a shot that lasts several seconds in near silence before the song starts. Michael Stipe, the lead singer of REM, sits near a pitcher of milk resting on a window ledge. A gentle rain falls outside. The camera tracks a couple of band members as they jog slowly in a semicircle in opposite directions, crossing paths and looking up in the air. The pitcher suddenly falls off the ledge, splattering milk across the floor.
>
> The scene foreshadows two interrelated themes in the video. First, the band members look heavenward to find a (fallen) Jesus, who eventually falls to earth. Second, the spilled milk raises critical questions: Should we cry over spilled milk? Is the loss of religion, of an institution, something to be mourned? What exactly have we lost? The milk represents religion; the spill indicates the liquidation of its authority in the lives of Xers. (p. 53)

Beaudoin continues his analysis by discussing in detail the significance of the representation of the Jesus who later falls from heaven in the video. This Jesus is represented as an old man, rather bewildered and at the mercy of those who wish to examine, mock or help him. At one point, this Jesus is also discovered to be wearing a grey wig, without which he looks even older and frailer. Beaudoin interprets these images as signs that the Jesus of traditional religion has become 'exhausted, worn out and sorry' and no longer able to command the devotion or hope of new generations (p. 67). As the video leaves us with an image of this old Jesus slumped on the ground, we return to a shot of Michael Stipe, behind whom is an open book framed by angelic wings. Beaudoin reads this as suggesting that – in the absence of a Jesus who could inspire us as a messiah – the Church instead gives the Bible a divine status, elevating its teaching and doctrine to a status beyond that attained by the old and weary Jesus himself.

Whilst the video to 'Losing My Religion' could be seen simply as a negative critique of the symbols and beliefs of institutional Christianity, Beaudoin interprets it as expressing more positive religious sentiments. Indeed the Jesus represented in this video is arguably one with whom members of 'Generation X' are more easily able to identify. Beaudoin suggests that:

> 'Losing My Religion' is sympathetic; there is a human sadness about this fallen Jesus, a disappointment that we can't make him be what he is supposed to be. Yet in that failure to live up to what the Church has made him, we understand him. He is with us, down on the ground, fallen from the sky, where he was out of our reach. Like the uncanny scene in the video, we are caught somewhere between the binding and releasing of Jesus, which has everything to do with Xers' own uncertainty about our freedom and captivity in contemporary culture . . . I am even tempted to say that Jesus has let the institution down and that the Church has capitalized on a Jesus they do not really seem to know. (p. 69)

The video to 'Losing My Religion' can therefore be interpreted as carrying more than a message about the irrelevance of the institutional Church in contemporary culture. It expresses a wistful longing for meaning, and depicts a figure of Jesus which, in his frailty and uncertainty, is one with whom members of 'Generation X' can identify. Far, then, from being simply a negative attack on the Church, the video to 'Losing My Religion' expresses something of the attitudes and beliefs of the 'Xers' who watch and appreciate it.

In Beaudoin's opinion, then, music videos (and other forms of popular culture) become the 'religious' texts through which members of 'Generation X' reflect about the meaning of existence. For Beaudoin's 'Xer', MTV becomes Scripture and the style of fashion that people choose becomes their personal statement about the nature of themselves and the world.

Now, in thinking about Beaudoin's argument, we may be sceptical about his idea of 'Generation X' as a generational cohort for all the reasons that we examined back in chapter 2. But even if we abandon the idea that 'Generation X' is a group of people of a certain age, and see a 'Generation X' attitude more in terms of the desire to pursue personal meaning beyond pre-packaged and marketed truths, then Beaudoin's argument could still have some validity. For if individuals within contemporary Western society are pursuing personally authentic meaning, is it not possible that popular culture is, as Beaudoin suggests, an essential resource for this quest? I think that Beaudoin's basic assertion about the significance of popular culture for the contemporary search for meaning is a very important one, but that on closer scrutiny there are problems with his idea of popular culture as a set of 'religious' texts. In the rest of this chapter, we will start to look at some of the difficulties with Beaudoin's approach and, in doing so, begin to consider some other ways in which people may be making use of popular culture in the contemporary world.

Caught in *The Matrix* – some problems with 'popular culture as Scripture'

Beaudoin's idea of popular culture functioning as some kind of Scripture may have some initial appeal, but on closer examin-

ation there are a number of problems with this idea. Firstly, we
need to think seriously about the extent to which popular cultural
'texts' do actually have clear and stable meanings that might
shape or express people's religious sentiments. Although Beaudoin seems to allow for the fact that people will interpret films,
music and fashion in different ways, he does also seem to maintain the belief that these popular cultural 'texts' do have core
meanings that convey a clear theological message. To examine
Beaudoin's assumption more critically here, we will turn our
attention to one of the most successful films produced in America
in recent years, *The Matrix*.

The Matrix, directed by Andy and Larry Wachowski, was
released in 1999. Based on a cartoon book, the film is set two
hundred years into the future when Artificial Intelligence
machines now control what is left of a war-ravaged world. To
maintain a regular energy source, these machines 'farm' humans
and keep them enclosed in cubicles in which they are able to
draw energy from them. To prevent any disruption to this
process, these human 'batteries' are connected up to a computer-
generated virtual reality (the Matrix) in which they believe they
are living in the 1990s. Under the mental illusion of living
ordinary lives, the majority of the human race is thus reduced
to being an imprisoned and passive energy source.

The central story-line of the film concerns a small group of
humans who live outside of the influence of the Matrix. This
group helps to free one man, Thomas Anderson (or 'Neo') from
the illusion of the Matrix in the belief that Neo is the one person
who has the potential to break its power. As the film progresses,
Neo's understanding changes from initial disbelief about the
existence of the Matrix, through learning to begin to influence
his environment in the Matrix, to the conclusion where he dies
and returns to life in the Matrix with renewed power to control
it. By the end of the film, the human race is still largely enslaved
within the illusion of the Matrix, but the presence of Neo within
it provides hope that its influence may now be diminishing.

In terms of examining Beaudoin's notion of popular culture as
Scripture, *The Matrix* is a particularly interesting case study as the
film is littered with religious images and ideas. Neo's death and
resurrection is central to his emergence as the Chosen One who

is able to control the Matrix. Morpheus, the leader of the rebel group, states his faith in Neo as the Chosen One in a way that is strongly reminiscent of John the Baptist's relation to Jesus. The idea of ordinary life as an illusion has clear affinities with Buddhist and Hindu notions of the illusory nature of what we take to be reality. The names of characters and places also have religious connotations. Morpheus' deputy is called Trinity, and the last surviving human city is called Zion. Furthermore the film can be seen as raising issues that are of fundamental concern to theological and philosophical reflection: what is the nature of truth? How can we learn the truth? What prevents us from understanding truth? To what extent are we truly free? What is the purpose of our lives? Is there more to life beyond the mundane level of our day-to-day existence?

Given the strong presence of religious images and theological questions and themes within this film, we might expect (according to Beaudoin's view) that the film conveys some clear message that might express or shape the religious sentiments of its many interested viewers. On closer inspection, however, it becomes clear that individual viewers have interpreted the 'religious' meaning of the film in radically different ways.

Consider the following assessment of the theological significance of *The Matrix*:

> On first hearing about the film one might think it carried Christian overtones, but the core message is pure new age philosophy. Like *Star Wars*, *Star Trek*, and many other Sci-fi/Spi-fi films, this one is a powerfully dangerous vehicle used to evangelize our culture with Eastern religious beliefs.
>
> The central theme teaches that the world we see around us is not real. It is an *illusion*. And that salvation comes through realizing and knowing about this illusion. Once someone realizes this supposed 'truth', then they are free to exercise miraculous, god-like powers and overcome the hidden authorities that have been controlling their lives.
>
> These beliefs are identical to the new age, gnostic philosophies I once followed before submitting to Jesus Christ. Hinduism for example teaches that the visible world is an illusion called 'maya', which keeps us in bondage. Salvation

in that system is possible only through realizing this *truth* and the fact that your real Self can break free and become its own authority. This insidious message originated with Lucifer and was seductively fed to Eve in the Garden of Eden. 'You shall become like gods' . . . As technology continues to improve and produce 'exciting' special effect movies like *The Matrix*, Lucifer's ability to con the world will increase exponentially. Please protect your teens and warn your friends about these subtle, insidious messages, which are so toxic to their souls. (Soulcare, 2002)

This critique of *The Matrix* as offering a 'non-Christian', 'New Age' spirituality is directly contradicted by other websites that offer detailed discussions of the implicit Christian theology within the film. One site, titled 'The Matrix as Messiah Movie', argues that the figure of Neo in the film is intended to be a modern-day representation of Jesus Christ (Awesomehouse, 2002). The authors of this site make their case by highlighting a number of parallels that they see between the film and the gospels' accounts of Jesus' life. These parallels vary from the more self-evident (Neo as the 'Chosen One' foretold by prophecy, his death and resurrection, and his 'ascension' at the end of the film) to the decidedly subtle (e.g. the seventy-two seconds on screen in which Neo is dead representing the seventy-two hours that Jesus was buried in the tomb). Other sites move beyond seeing *The Matrix* as a retelling of the Gospel story to suggesting that it reflects Christian theological ideas in more diffuse ways. Thus the process of being freed from the illusion of the Matrix could be likened to the process of being 'born again' and freed from the influence of the principalities and powers that oppose human welfare (cf. Ephesians 6:12). Furthermore the choice to fight the Matrix rather than to return to its comfortable illusion (as one of the characters, Cypher, attempts to do), can be seen as an assertion of the importance of positive moral choices over apathy and nihilism (Xenos, 2002).

Disagreement over the 'religious' or 'theological' meaning of the film does not focus simply on whether it seeks to convey some kind of Christian orthodoxy or not. Another website argues that its central meaning does not relate primarily to the ideas of any of the major world religions, but to occult insights discovered by the writer Carlos Castenada:

> Reading Carlos Castenada's last work . . . , *The Active Side of Infinity,* may well send a chill of recognition down the spine of anyone who has seen *The Matrix* . . . In Castenada's final work, Don Juan Matus introduces Carlos to the sorcerers' 'topic of topics': the existence of a dark predatorial force that has enslaved humanity, in order to farm it as a food source. This force, or entity, he calls the flyer, describing it as 'a predator that came from the depths of the cosmos and took over the rule of our lives. Human beings are its prisoners. The predator is our lord and master. It has rendered us docile, helpless . . . They took us over because we were food for them and they squeeze us mercilessly because we are their sustenance . . .'
>
> When Don Juan states all this flatly to Carlos as an 'energetic fact', Carlos' reaction is uncannily akin to that of Neo in the movie, following Morpheus' essentially identical revelation. ' "No, no," I heard myself saying. "This is absurd. What you are saying is monstrous. It simply can't be true." Don Juan asks simply, "Why not? Because it infuriates you?" ' (Wynd, 2002)

It is evident just from this small sample of websites that *The Matrix* is being interpreted here in radically different ways. From propaganda for 'New Age' philosophy, through retelling of the Christian gospel, to representation about the occult truth underlying our existence, these 'readings' of the 'text' of the film result in highly diverse interpretations of its narrative and symbolism. The way in which *The Matrix* is viewed and understood by its audience becomes even more complex, however, if we realise that these websites have a particular interest in exploring the 'religious' significance of the film. In one of my undergraduate classes, I encouraged the group to discuss the meaning of *The Matrix*. It became clear that amongst these students, who were all studying theology and were thus more sensitised to religious ideas and imagery than many people, the vast majority had not perceived any religious significance to *The Matrix* at all on their first viewing of it. Indeed, for most of them, it had been enjoyable simply as a stylish science-fiction action film. Not only, then, do viewers interpret the religious significance of its narrative and symbols in different ways, but many do not recognise any religious symbols or themes in the film at all.

This survey of different audience 'readings' of *The Matrix* suggests that we should be careful not to adopt a naïve view of popular culture 'texts' as Scripture. It is evident from such a film that popular culture does not simply carry clear meanings that shape the way in which people view life. Rather the interests and commitments that individuals have will shape their understanding of the popular cultural 'texts' that they read, hear or see (see, e.g., Storey, 1999, p. 79). An individual with strong conservative Evangelical Christian convictions is therefore likely to understand the meaning of *The Matrix* differently to an individual with strong Buddhist convictions. Similarly a person viewing the film with a strong interest in science-fiction as a means of exploring important issues about our existence will tend to perceive it differently to someone who chooses to see it because he or she wants to watch something stylish and mainstream whilst on a first date. The idea that popular culture could function as a stable resource of meanings that help inform our understanding of life is thus somewhat dubious.

This diversity in people's interpretation of and response to popular culture has attracted significant interest within the field of cultural studies. One of the leading theorists to have discussed the ways in which people make use of popular culture in everyday life is Michel de Certeau. In his seminal book *The Practice of Everyday Life*, de Certeau (1984) argues that whilst the majority of people have little direct control over the design and creation of the popular cultural products that they consume, they retain considerable freedom in the way in which they make use of those products. De Certeau likens this freedom in relation to popular culture to the practice of what, in France, is known as 'la perruque' (or 'the wig'). 'La perruque' is a term used to refer to a situation in which workers disguise their own work or activity as that of their employer. One common example of this, in an age in which many offices have online computer facilities, are instances where workers will use office time to send emails to friends or to browse websites that interest them. On the face of it, the employees are diligently working at their desk, but in reality they are turning the resources of their office to meet their own personal interests rather than fulfilling the purpose of the employer.

Just as employees can use the resources of their employer in ways that their employer does not intend, so consumers of popular culture can make use of popular culture in ways that may not have been intended by those who have created or marketed it. De Certeau (1984) thus suggests that ordinary individuals have 'countless ways of refusing to accord the established order the status of a law, a meaning or a fatality' (p. 26). In other words, individuals have a wide variety of ways of subverting the intended meanings of popular cultural 'texts' and using them to serve their own interests and commitments. The following examples illustrate a range of possibilities. Fans of a particular film or TV programme can create new stories and plot-lines for it and publish these in fanzines, so that the 'official story' of *Star Wars* or *Twin Peaks* becomes embellished with new stories not created by the official authors (see Jenkins, 1992, p. 73). Similarly viewers can treat a popular cultural 'text' ironically. The films of 1950s Hollywood director, Ed Wood, have thus achieved cult status amongst some people not because of their interesting or inspirational plot-lines, but precisely because the films are produced so badly with poor acting, shoddy special effects and major continuity mistakes. What viewers celebrate in Ed Wood's films is thus generally different to what Wood himself intended. Alternatively, the meaning of a popular cultural 'text' can be 'misread' in highly creative ways. Thus, for example, Afrika Bambaata, one of the originators of hip-hop decided to call his collective the 'Zulu Nation', having seen the 1964 film *Zulu* starring Michael Caine. The film itself was primarily concerned with depicting the courage of a small group of white British soldiers who successfully defended themselves against a Zulu army at Rorke's Drift. As such, the film contained an implicit defence of British imperialism. Bambaata, however, chose to view the film as an example of a black African popular movement that rose up to take control of its destiny, and through doing this named and inspired a collective that engaged in a number of community projects in black communities in New York.

These examples clearly illustrate David Lyon's observation that 'once the text is out in the open, it is extended by others' interpretations, spiralling endlessly beyond all efforts to tether the text to truth or to fix its meaning in place' (1994, p. 18). To think of popular culture as a series of 'texts' that convey meanings about our lives may therefore be too simplistic. Certainly popular culture does not function as a source of meaning that we, as viewers, listeners, readers or consumers, passively receive.[3] Rather we engage actively with popular culture, and the way in which we interpret or 'read' it will be shaped as much (if not more) by the interests, taste, beliefs and commitments that we already have than by anything that is in the popular cultural 'text' itself.[4]

The idea that popular cultural 'texts' might function as some kind of Scripture for people in contemporary Western society needs to be treated carefully then. It seems unlikely that popular cultural 'texts' will typically convey some clear meaning that will be passively assimilated by those who see, listen, read or buy it. Rather, if popular culture is a source of meaning to individuals it is because they engage actively with it, interpreting it in conventional or surprising (but always personal) ways, and weaving it into larger patterns of meaning in their lives. Popular culture may not be the Scripture that provides meaning to a passive audience, but a complex and colourful array of building blocks out of which individuals may construct part of their understanding of life.

Beyond popular culture as 'text': the roles of popular culture in everyday life

It may be, however, that we need to be cautious not only about the idea that popular cultural 'texts' convey clear meanings, but even about the very idea of popular culture as 'text' itself. Janice Radway, who has previously undertaken a major study of the significance of romantic novels for a sample of female readers (see Radway, 1987), has since questioned the validity of studies which try to establish the meaning of specific 'texts' for a particular audience. She has argued that such studies begin with the assumption that there are specific 'texts' (whether Mills & Boon novels, a particular soap opera, or a specific film) that are meaningful to those who consume them, and which then try to establish what this meaning is for the audience. This approach has a certain clarity and appeal for researchers who are used to reading, thinking about and interpreting texts. In practice, though, people in daily life may not perceive these popular cultural products as 'texts' at all. By focusing on the idea of popular cultural products as 'texts', we therefore run the risk of imposing a view of popular culture that is actually quite alien to the function that popular culture serves in many people's lives. Rather than trying to interpret the meaning of popular cultural 'texts', Radway suggests that we might do better to study more broadly the different functions that popular culture can have in everyday life (see Storey, 1999, pp. 124f.).

Within the field of cultural studies, a range of functions have been identified for popular culture beyond that of providing 'texts' for interpretation. We can summarise some of these main functions as follows:

- **Popular culture can be a focus for social interaction**. For example, one *Star Trek* fan has commented that people attend 'Trekkie' conventions and take part in other 'Trekkie' activities precisely because 'we enjoy each other's company' (Jenkins, 1992, p. 75). Thus, whilst the content of *Star Trek* programmes and films will hold innate interest for these fans, this shared interest in *Star Trek* is also a means to an end of enjoyable social interaction. The image of the 'Royle Family' or 'The Simpsons' sitting around their television set is another example of how popular culture can become a focus for conversation and social interaction.

- **Popular culture can be a means of escapism from ordinary 'real life' experiences.** Radway, for example, comments that, for some women, reading romance fiction offers them the possibility of entering imaginatively into another world that is set apart from their ordinary world of problems and responsibilities (Storey, 1999, p. 101). In addition to this imaginative escapism, the very act of going to an exciting physical location (such as a club, sports venue, cinema or theme park) can also serve as a means of escaping more mundane forms of day-to-day life.

- **Popular culture can be a means by which people communicate about their 'real world' experiences.** One researcher has reported a conversation she overheard in which four women were discussing their grandchildren and then began to discuss recent events in *Coronation Street*. The discussion of their families and the discussion of events in the soap opera became seamlessly blended together to the extent where the lives of characters in the soap opera became a focus for these women to discuss problems they were facing in their own lives (Storey, 1999, p. 110). Popular culture can therefore provide a platform for conversation in which more intimate 'real world' concerns can be discussed and explored.

Popular culture can therefore serve a range of important functions in everyday life. If people devote significant time and energy into popular cultural activities or products, we cannot simply assume that this is because popular culture is serving as a 'text' that helps them make sense of life. Although Beaudoin may well be right to assert that the 'Generation X' phenomenon is closely associated with popular culture, the reasons why people enthusiastically engage with popular culture may not primarily be because it functions as a kind of Scripture for them.

We have noted two reasons, then, why Beaudoin's notion of popular culture as 'religious text' is open to criticism. Firstly, it is evident that, far from conveying clear and consistent meanings, popular cultural 'texts' are open to all kinds of interpretations and responses based on the particular beliefs, values, interests and commitments of the reader. Furthermore, popular culture has a broad range of functions in everyday life and we cannot assume that people's interest in it shows that it helps them to make sense of life. Taken together these two points suggest that Beaudoin's approach of trying to provide 'theological' interpretations of popular cultural 'texts' may not be the most productive way of trying to understand the significance of popular culture in people's search for personal meaning. In contrast to Beaudoin's interest with the popular cultural 'text' itself, it would seem far more productive (as Radway suggests) to explore the significance that popular culture has in people's ordinary, lived experience. By studying its uses and meaning for people, we may get a clearer picture of how (and to what extent) individuals use popular culture to make sense of life than if we simply focus on what we think the message of popular cultural 'texts' might be. In the following chapter we will adopt such an approach by beginning to explore whether clubbing has a religious significance in the lives of people committed to club culture.

5
Is There a 'Clubbing Spirituality'?

> This is my Church
> This is where I heal my hurts . . .
> For tonight
> God is a DJ

This line from the dance track 'God is a DJ' by the band Faithless is well known in club culture, almost to the point of becoming a cliché. But is there any substance to this idea that clubs are becoming new churches for people, or that dance music via the DJ is becoming an important new experience of transcendence? Is there such a thing as a 'clubbing spirituality'? This chapter will aim to begin to answer these questions, as well as exploring why these are worthwhile questions to ask in the first place.

In the previous chapter we saw that people can interpret and make use of popular culture in surprising and original ways as they seek to find and express what is meaningful and important to them. Trying to identify 'religious' or 'theological' themes in films, novels, pop songs, TV programmes or computer games can have some value in helping us to reflect about the meaning and value of our existence. But if we simply study popular cultural 'texts' or events at this theoretical level and do not examine what personal significance people actually draw from them in real-life situations, then we risk missing out on understanding the complex ways in which popular culture can really be a source of meaning. In this chapter, therefore, we will attempt to begin to answer our questions about the existence of a clubbing spirituality by finding out what some clubbers themselves have to say about their clubbing experiences and the meaning that these hold for them.[1]

Before we move on to hear what clubbers themselves have to say, it will be important first of all to give an explanation about why this kind of study of club culture seems appropriate or relevant. Why would we even think that club culture might be a new form of 'religion' or that there might be something like a 'clubbing spirituality'?

Club culture as a source of meaning and transformative experience

There is no question that club culture has been one of the most significant developments in popular culture for young people in Britain and more gradually in the United States over the past decade or so. The contemporary club scene has important roots in the rave movement of the late 1980s in which an emerging style of electronic dance music from Chicago, 'acid house', combined with the increasing availability and use of the recreational drug Ecstasy to create an entirely new kind of dance experience (see Collin, 1997). This successful blend of a repetitive rhythmic music with a recreational drug that provided both a heightened awareness of the music and a sense of closeness to other people led to an explosion in rave events. These events could attract several thousand people in some cases and were often held outdoors or (legally or illegally) in large industrial buildings such as warehouses or aircraft hangars. By 1993, the total attendance at rave events in Britain was estimated to be 50 million people (Parker *et al.*, 1998), and rave events were also spreading across North America from the clubs of New York to the full moon beach parties of San Francisco (Silcott, 2000). Raves became a global phenomenon with events being held in places as diverse as Toronto, Cape Town, Goa, Berlin, Tokyo and Ko Pha-Ngan in Thailand. In the 1990s, the success of the rave movement combined with pressures to bring it under a tighter legal framework (particularly in Britain) led to the emergence of smaller clubs in which the ethos of new forms of dance music combined with recreational drug use was maintained. This new club scene continued to be hugely successful with more than £2bn being spent by British clubbers on their nights out in 1996 (Malbon, 1999). Over time some of the new generation of clubs, such as the Ministry of Sound, Gatecrasher and Cream, have themselves become global brands which offer not only a range of club nights, but also release their own dance music CDs, publish their own magazines and even offer travel services. The new club culture of the past decade, then, has certainly transformed the popular music scene – Silcott (2000) notes that in the United States in the late 1990s turntables used by DJs consistently outsold electric guitars. But the significance of this new club scene extends far beyond a new fashion in electronically generated music. Clubbing has become a global culture and industry in which potentially millions of young people participate (see, e.g., theworldparty, 2002), and which has had an effect on fashion, the media and even the way in which mainstream brands choose to advertise or depict themselves (see Bucknole, 2000).

Clearly, then, the emergence of a global club scene has been an important trend in popular culture over the past decade. It may be harder, though, to see at first glance why we might want to think about this movement as having any 'religious' or 'theological' significance. After all, survey evidence can be cited that indicates that many clubbers report that they go clubbing primarily because they find it an enjoyable and sociable experience (Malbon, 1999, p. 9). It could therefore be argued that clubbing is a significant and popular cultural activity simply because it is the best entertainment format on the market (Collin, 1997, p. 4). Whilst the idea that clubbing is popular because it is an enjoyable leisure activity cannot be dismissed, there is evidence that for at least some young adults it does function as a significant source of meaning in their lives.

One strand of this evidence comes from writers who suggest that club culture can offer a ritual framework in which an important form of spiritual or transcendent experience becomes possible. Russell Newcombe, for example, describes rave events in the following way:

> Raving can be viewed as a transcendental mind-altering

experience providing psychic relief to alienated people in a secular, repressive and materialistic society. Ecstasy and other drugs are the keys that unlock the doors to these desired states of consciousness . . . a deeply desired escape from the constraints of the self and normal behaviour. To stretch the religious metaphor, DJs are the high priests of the rave ceremony, responding to the mood of the crowd, with their mixing desks symbolizing the altar (the only direction in which ravers consistently face). Dancing at raves may be construed as the method by which ravers 'worship' the God of altered consciousness. (Saunders *et al.*, 2000, p. 168)

A similar point is made by Simon Reynolds (1998) who draws analogies between club culture and early pagan mystery rites that were held in near darkness involving mass chanting, dancing and the use of hallucinogenics (pp. 408f.). Nicholas Saunders also tells the story of a Buddhist monk whom he took to a rave and who felt at home in that event because he recognised it as a form of meditation (Saunders *et al.*, 2000, p. 176). Certainly if we see contemporary club culture as a mass movement in which people come together in order to experience altered states of consciousness, then it is hard to think of similar movements historically which have not had some kind of religious significance or dimension to them.

A small number of clubs explicitly acknowledge a spiritual or religious dimension to their events. The London club Return to the Source describes its events in the following way:

The all night dance ritual is a memory that runs deep within us all; a memory that takes us back to a time when people had respect for our great mother earth and each other. Dancing was our rite of passage, our shamanic journey into altered states of reality where we embodied the Great Spirit and the magic of life. We danced around great fires, we chanted and we drummed, empowering ourselves and our community. Then the religions of fear began to take hold. They destroyed our dance rituals, burning all who dared to question the new order. However, the power could not be suppressed forever and the great cycles of time have brought us full circle to this moment where we are gathering once again. The ancient memory has reawakened, the all-night dance ritual has returned.

At Return to the Source, it is our vision to bring back the dance ritual. A ritual is a sacred act with focused intention. We aim to create a modern day positive space, created with love where we can join as one tribe to journey deep into trance, just as our ancestors did. (rtts, 2002)

Although such a detailed and explicit recognition of a spiritual or religious dimension of clubbing tends to be in the minority, it is still striking how often religious images are used more generally within club culture by those involved in producing dance music and by club promoters. The lyrics of the dance-track 'God is a DJ' by the group Faithless, cited at the beginning of this chapter, are a good example of the use of traditional religious language in relation to clubbing experiences. In addition to its use by vocalists, it is also not uncommon for dance music to feature samples of religious songs or evangelistic sermons (e.g. 'Matthew 16' by Dale & Caesar). Journalists and other writers commenting on dance culture have also employed religious language or imagery. The cover of the June 2000 issue of *DJ* magazine proclaimed the dance musician and DJ, Paul van Dyk, to be the 'Trance Messiah'. Similarly in an article on dance culture for a cultural studies reader, the DJ Dave Haslam (1997) has claimed that 'DJ-ing is evangelism: a desire to share songs'.

The use of religious discourse is also evident amongst some club promoters. A number of clubs have directly derived their name from religious language: God's Kitchen, The House of God, and Salvation being examples of these. Religious images are also evident in more detailed ways in publicity materials promoting clubs or dance music. The website for the Ministry of Sound, one of the emerging global club brands, recently included the following news item:

Intent on spreading the gospel of dance music beyond the realms of the initiated, an evangelical posse of top UK dance acts have announced plans to spread the good beat across the uncharted land of philistine rock worshippers throughout North America. With a few pockets of dance missionaries and converts already baptising the willing in

small underground pockets across this great spiritual waste-
land, the dance powers that be have decided it is time to
convert the mass majority of rock heathens to the true faith
and save them from the damnation that results from a life
wasted on country and western or prog rock. Hallelujah!
Rejoice America your salvation is nearly upon you! (Ministry
of Sound, 2000)

The religious discourse employed here is clearly heavily ironic,
yet this does not mean that such use of religious imagery is
without significance. Indeed, it can be understood as an attempt
by some of those involved in the creation and maintenance of
the club scene to convey the idea that club culture is a serious
source of meaning and value for people who participate in it.
When religious images are used in relation to clubbing, then,
the intention is not to make any particularly serious or specific
theological claims, but rather to make the point that club culture
has largely replaced traditional forms of religion as a source of
identity and meaning in the lives of young people. This was
illustrated by the Chief Executive of the Ministry of Sound, Mark
Rodol, who defended his company's bid to take over the 'Spirit
Zone' in the London Millennium Dome by saying: 'We're disillusioned with religion: television, the Internet and the Ministry
of Sound have replaced it' (Taylor, 1998). Much the same point
was made in a television interview with Mike McKay, co-owner
of the Ibizan super-club Manumission, when he claimed that 'if
Christianity has been around for two thousand years, there's no
reason why Manumission shouldn't be around for two thousand
years as well.'

The use of religious imagery in club culture could therefore
be interpreted as an indication of the significance that clubbing
holds for some people. At the same time, some caution may
need to be taken with such an interpretation when the 'religious'
significance of clubbing is being talked up by club promoters
such as Mark Rodol who have a vested financial interest in the
maintenance and growth of the club scene. Further evidence of
the club scene as a source of meaning can be gained, however,
from attending to clubbers' own accounts of their experiences.

Some of these accounts clearly depict clubbing as having a

transformative effect on the individual clubber's life. Tanya, a contributor to Melissa Harrison's anthology *High Society* (1998) writes the following:

> I had my first E experience when I was twenty-five, just a couple of years ago. It has led to many personal and spiritual experiences which have changed my life for the better . . . I can remember that first time watching people bonding on and off the dance floor, watching friends and strangers embrace, and I felt amazed and elated, and thought how right it seemed. A stranger caught my smile, and instead of stonewalling me, he smiled right back, and at that moment I felt my natural love for others bubble up as I lost my barriers of fear. I found that night that I was able to tell my friends how much I loved and valued them, and I could make connections with many other people because I had lost my usual mistrust of strangers. (Harrison, 1998, p. 26)

Tanya's experience is echoed in the following extract from a commentary on a night in a club by Ben Malbon, who has conducted one of the most substantial participant-observation studies of the club scene in Britain:

> There came a point when I was just taken aback by what I was witnessing . . . Some extraordinary empathy was at work in that crowd, particularly when at the kind of extended climax of the evening the music and lighting effects combined so powerfully with the moving crowd on the dance floor. Clubbers were losing it all over the place. This kind of context – this sound and lightscape – must surely change the ways that people interact. I mean, people are just so close to each other; proximately and emotionally. The clubbers were sharing something precious, something personal, something enriching. The intensity of this fusion of motions and emotions was almost overwhelming. (Malbon, 1999, p. xii)

In these statements from Tanya and Ben Malbon we gain some sense of the power of clubbing experiences which transcend 'normal' social experiences, and which may be interpreted by clubbers as having a transformative effect on their lives. Within clubbers' accounts of these intense, transformative experiences, two major themes can be noted. Firstly, some people describe these experiences as involving a transformed experience of self. One of Malbon's interviewees, Valerie, makes the following observation:

> 'I believe that we all have different personas, yeah [uh-huh, right]. So you're a totally different person with me than you are with your mother [oh, definitely!]. Right, and . . . I think I like to believe that when I'm on an E I have no defences whatsoever, so in many ways I would say that the person I am when I'm on an E is the "real me" right, because I feel totally open and . . . I feel clean, yeah . . . I feel cleansed of all my worldly woes . . . I don't, I feel like, I trust, I feel more trusting, I'm quite a trusting person anyway, yeah. I don't . . . it's really difficult – I feel really sort of spiritual like I don't judge, I trust, I feel cleansed, I feel . . . it's like a really sort of pure feeling.' (Malbon, 1999, p. 126)

This sense of connecting with oneself in a deeper way through clubbing was also echoed by Paul, one of the clubbers that I have interviewed:[2]

> 'If I'm dancing and I close my eyes, then everything else is gone and it's just me. Especially when you're dancing, you feel every movement you make. Sometimes you're aware of every thought you're having. You're much more aware of yourself.'

In addition to a transformed sense of self, some clubbers also report a transformed sense of relationship to other people. This is evident, for example, in the quotation from Tanya given above. It also arose as a theme in my interview with Paul and Beth:

> PAUL: 'You share something [in the club] in terms of experience . . .'
>
> BETH: ' . . . That makes you closer . . . the intensity of experience, of having a really good time together . . .'
>
> PAUL: ' . . . Saying things to each other that wouldn't normally be said, nice things that wouldn't normally be said, nice things that people wouldn't normally say to each

other because they shouldn't, things that you think but you think you shouldn't say. Like male friends saying that they find you attractive, things that you'd normally be embarrassed to say . . .'

BETH: ' . . . Blokes would go round hugging each other . . .'

PAUL: ' . . . Things that would normally make you a little bit careful in social situations, you don't mind doing.'

This notion of a deeper connection with others through clubbing is extended further by Malbon's notion of the significant role of 'oceanic' or 'ecstatic' experiences in the club scene. Drawing on the work of Laski (1961), Malbon (1999) argues that at its most intense the clubbing experience becomes oceanic in the sense that individual clubbers lose their sense of individual selfhood and experience themselves as part of a greater whole. As with all of the transformative aspects of clubbing noted here, such experiences are often, though not always, connected to the use of recreational drugs. Malbon thus describes as 'ecstatic' those oceanic experiences that occur for people as a result of their use of the drug Ecstasy, the effects of which can include a deeper experience of empathic connection with others (see also Hammersley *et al.*, 2002).

Whilst, at first glance then, club culture may simply seem to be another growing part of the global entertainment and leisure industry, there is some evidence that it should be explored as a potentially important popular cultural source of meaning for many people. We may or may not accept the direct analogies that some writers have drawn between raves and religious experiences and rituals. But the fact that so much energy and commitment is invested in club culture by clubbers and that some do report their clubbing experiences as having a trans-formative element to them, means that there are good grounds for being curious about what significance clubbing really holds for people. In the remainder of this chapter, we will now look at what a small group of clubbers have to say about how they interpret their clubbing experiences. This in turn will help us think more about the role of popular culture in people's search for, and expression of, meaning in their lives.

The meaning of clubbing experiences: hearing clubbers' own perspectives

Through conducting individual interviews with a small group of clubbers (see note 2), I tried to understand what their clubbing experiences meant for them and whether they perceived any particular religious or spiritual element in these experiences. Two striking themes emerged from these interviews. Firstly, the clubbers that I spoke to did not generally understand their clubbing experiences to be important because they had a religious or spiritual element to them. Secondly, these clubbers tended to interpret their clubbing experiences in highly diverse ways that reflected more general values and beliefs that they held. Let us see how these themes emerged from what they had to say.

Firstly, then, it was clear that the majority of the interviewees did not see clubbing as a spiritual or religious experience, and that none of them saw clubbing as a primary source of spirituality for themselves. Indeed, for most of the participants, to view clubbing in such terms was seen as immature, unbalanced or lacking in critical thought. This was demonstrated when I asked these clubbers what they thought about people using terms such as 'religious' or 'spiritual' in relation to clubbing experiences. For example:

> GORDON: 'Some people have talked, and this is one of the things that I'm interested in as well, some people have talked about that kind of experience, or like the experience of dancing like that, as almost being a religious or a spiritual experience. I mean, would that mean anything to you or would you agree with that?'
>
> LOUISE: 'Um, no, not really. I don't think so, um . . . No, I think it's just something that you like doing, so you do it, do you know what I mean? I wouldn't say it's religious or anything like that. I mean if you'd asked me when I was eighteen I might have agreed. You know, but, no, I'm older and wiser now and I don't agree with that . . . When

I was about eighteen I was really naïve, and I did think that's all it was about, and, you know, that was it.'

For Louise, therefore, viewing clubbing in religious or spiritual terms is something that she might have done when she was a few years younger, before she was 'older and wiser'. As we will see a bit later on, her understanding of clubbing is heavily influenced by a 'developmental narrative' in which she regards being absorbed by the club scene as a valuable experience, but one which over time she has grown out of. Seeing clubbing as 'religious' in its significance is, therefore, to Louise, a symptom of an insufficiently mature perspective on life.

In my interview with Paul and Beth a negative view of thinking of clubbing as a 'religion' or source of spirituality was evident, though for different reasons:

GORDON: 'Some people talk about clubbing, and in particular the experience of dancing, as being like a religious or a spiritual experience. I mean, does that description mean anything to you, or would you agree with it, or . . .?'

PAUL: 'I wouldn't describe it as a religious experience. There've been times when I might start to think that maybe I was experiencing something more than [tape unclear], but I don't know if that was something outside of me or inside me. I don't think I'd like to call it spiritual.'

BETH: 'I wouldn't either.'

PAUL: 'I think it's more a case of unlocking things inside you, inside of you rather than outside of you.'

GORDON: 'Right, so is that about the idea that to use the word "spiritual" there would sort of imply a God or something "out there" [Paul: Yeah] that was connecting with you, which seems quite alien to your experience? [Paul: Yeah]'

BETH: 'If you hadn't said that I would never have thought. It would just never have occurred to me.'

PAUL: 'There have been times when I've come off the dance floor and sort of thought to myself, "Is this the way to sort of find meaning and stuff?" But then always the next day I'll wake up and think, "No, I was just having a really, really good time." And I don't think there's really anything more to it. I think a lot of people read a lot of things into it, especially people who take a lot of drugs. And then they have such a good time that they think there must be something more behind it.'

Again neither Paul nor Beth regard it useful or meaningful to think about clubbing in spiritual or religious terms. For Beth it seems entirely outside of her normal horizon of meaning to think about clubbing as being in any sense a spiritual or religious activity, and she seems actively opposed to viewing it in these terms (her statement 'I wouldn't either' was spoken with some feeling). Paul, on the other hand, has considered the possibility that clubbing involves a transcendent element, but has rejected this idea. Instead he believes that attributing spiritual significance to clubbing is a product of reading too much into a very powerful and enjoyable experience. For Paul, those who see clubbing as having a profound spiritual significance are guilty of, at best, an insufficiently critical approach to their experience or, worse, some form of self-deception. Interestingly Paul's rejection of the word 'spiritual' arises out of his assumption that 'spiritual' implies connection with some external transcendent being or force. The characteristically New Age principle of 'self-spirituality' (Heelas, 1996), in which one seeks to discover that which is god within oneself, has evidently not influenced his thinking.

One further reason for rejecting the notion of clubbing as a significant source of spirituality was given by another inter-viewee, Rob. Rob offered the following observation about those who use religious or spiritual imagery in relation to clubbing:

> ROB: 'And I think she [Sheryl Garratt, author of *Adventures in Wonderland*] does use quite kind of, not prophetic, but very sort of utopian imagery and stuff, and I think that's probably quite a product of the drugs involved. Um, 'cos as I say, we're in kind of a, not post-ecstasy generation, but it's kind of like condoms came in and then they worked out and then they were just accepted as part of reality. And nobody gets embarrassed about going and buying condoms now. So like Ecstasy now is probably not so much the wonder-drug that it was in '92 or '89, in the "Wow! This is fantastic!", the "new life". And a lot of

people now are mixing and matching, and they're treating it as just another add-on and less of a spiritual journey.'

Rob therefore perceives the notion of clubbing as having a religious or spiritual significance as somewhat passé. He associates it with those people who were pioneers in the club scene and who were profoundly influenced by their first contacts with Ecstasy in the late 1980s and early 1990s when (according to 'club-lore' at least) the drug was widely available in much purer forms. For Rob and his contemporaries, then, the notion of a 'clubbing spirituality' is not personally meaningful because their lives are not primarily informed by the practices and discourses of club culture. Rather, for them, clubbing becomes something that is part of the 'mix' of a person's life, but not the central source of meaning for that life.

Interestingly, the only person in this sample who interpreted clubbing as having a spiritual significance viewed it in generally negative terms. One of my interviewees, Kath, had a clear Christian faith, which could be described as Evangelical and Charismatic. Kath's response to the question of thinking about clubbing in 'spiritual' or 'religious' terms was interesting and complex, and reflected tensions between her clubbing experiences and her religious views:

> KATH: 'I do feel that music is, is a, has spiritual dimensions. Um, I mainly feel that because in the Old Testament there are examples like when David played the lyre for Saul his demons were calmed. And that's what I try to base most of my judgements on, the Bible. So I do feel that. But also from experience there is that kind of, trying to explain why I dance to music is . . . It moves something that isn't just emotions, it is, and I can understand how people see the club experience as something spiritual, because the music is just, and the atmosphere . . . I would say it is very spiritual, but at the second hand I don't know I'd say it was spiritual in a good way, in a holy way. I think that there is a lot of darkness and otherness that does get in in that way, especially with things like the alcohol abuse, and substance abuse, the kind of mind expanding or detracting substances that, that allow other dimensions

in . . . other spiritual things to enter which aren't necessarily characterised by self-control and love and
gentleness which the things of God are.'

Kath's answer demonstrates a greater willingness to interpret
clubbing experiences in 'spiritual' terms. For Kath, though, the
word 'spiritual' alludes not only to an individual's core self, but
also to a cosmos inhabited by 'spiritual' forces which can be
either positive or harmful. She interprets clubbing as having
some spiritual significance for herself in a positive sense, for it
touches a part of her that is unmoved by verbal interactions. But
at the same time she sees it as a potential vehicle for damaging
'spiritual forces' which prey upon people who do not guard
against them or who indulge in risk activities such as alcohol
or substance abuse. Kath therefore demonstrates an intriguing
ambivalence towards clubbing to which we shall return shortly.

From these responses, then, it is clear that none of the participants regarded the discourses or practices of clubbing as a
primary source of personal spirituality. Most of the participants
took a negative view of describing clubbing in spiritual or
religious terms. In the case of Kath, who was the only person to
attribute 'spiritual' significance to clubbing, it was clear that
her spirituality was primarily shaped by Christian, rather than
'clubbing', ways of thinking about the world. In relation to the
question that we began with at the start of this chapter, then,
these interviews provided no real evidence of a distinctive 'clubbing spirituality'. This is not to suggest, though, that no clubbers
will interpret their clubbing experiences as having a spiritual or
religious significance for them. Indeed it was clear that Paul and
Rob were aware of people who would interpret clubbing in that
way. What these responses do suggest, though, is that we need
to be very careful about making generalised statements about
the 'religious' or 'spiritual' significance of the club scene when
people who take part in it do not perceive any religious or
spiritual elements to it themselves.

From my description of these interviews so far it could be
argued that the lack of evidence of a 'clubbing spirituality' is a
direct consequence of the phrasing of my interview questions.
By referring directly to clubbing as a 'spiritual' or 'religious'

experience, it could be argued that I have used terms that may be alien to many young adults and that are unlikely to connect with their experience. It could thus be argued that signs of a clubbing spirituality might be more evident at points in the interviews where the terms 'spiritual' and 'religious' are not employed, but where the participants were explaining how they made sense of, and what they valued in, their clubbing experiences. In reality, though, a broader view of the interviews reveals that whilst each of the participants clearly valued their clubbing experiences, each interpreted them in different ways based on different personal values and beliefs. At no point, therefore, was a common form of drawing meaning from clubbing experiences evident in these interviews.[3]

Space does not allow a detailed description of the ways in which each interviewee constructed and interpreted their clubbing experiences, but a brief comparison of three of the interviewees, Louise, Paul and Kath, will demonstrate these differences clearly.

As we noted above, Louise's interpretation of her clubbing experiences was based on a developmental narrative in which she saw love of clubbing primarily as a 'phase' that she went through in her late teens and early twenties. Linked with this was another, rather wistful narrative about how the exciting club scene that she had been involved in during the early 1990s had become more mainstream, commercialised and safe. Louise still regularly goes to clubs (at least once every two to three weeks), but saw the earlier period in her life as one in which she was preoccupied with clubbing – 'If I couldn't go clubbing, nothing seemed worthwhile.' Louise described this period as an exciting and adventurous one – 'You'd go out and you wouldn't know where you'd end up at the end of the night.' It was also a period in which she rebelled against parental expectations. She refused to get a job because she wanted to go clubbing in the week, and in the daytime she would socialise with the friends with whom she went clubbing. Her desire to go clubbing was so strong, she commented, that she would sometimes pawn her possessions so that she could afford a night out. Her view of clubbing has changed somewhat now, however. Although she still enjoys it she is starting to develop new and wider interests and is enjoying this: 'When I used to go clubbing I used to think that going out for a meal or something would be really boring – what's the point? – but now I love it.'

There are three elements that stand out from Louise's account of her clubbing experiences that indicate what she valued and found meaningful in it. Firstly, Louise highly valued the social element in clubbing. This was not only about enjoying herself with the close group of friends with whom she went out, but also about feeling part of a larger scene in which she regularly saw the same faces. Louise did not regard this wider clubbing community as being particularly close, but seeing the same people did give her a sense of belonging – she spoke of feeling like a 'proper clubber'. Secondly, Louise highly valued the sense of fun and adventure that she got through clubbing. For example, she described the atmosphere of a good night out in a club as 'really uplifting' and the feeling when the DJ plays a favourite track as like being at the top of a rollercoaster. Thirdly, Louise enjoys the broadly sexual atmosphere of clubs. She described how she enjoys it when men find her attractive and try to chat her up – 'It's nice to pull, means you've still got it.' Overall, Louise's attitude to clubbing could be summarised as one in which she values her clubbing experiences because they are sociable and entertaining.

A contrasting view is demonstrated by Kath. As we saw earlier, Kath has strong Christian beliefs and found clubbing to be an ambivalent experience for her. On the one hand there were certain things about clubbing that she found unique and invaluable. Dancing is very important to her because through it she experiences a significant aspect of herself that cannot be expressed verbally. The club is the only public space that Kath can find where she can express herself through dance – the only other places are dance classes which she finds too structured to allow free expression. Another aspect of clubbing that she highly values is that of sharing non-verbal experiences with friends. Although she is careful about whom she makes eye contact with on the dance floor, she enjoys holding the gaze of friends whilst dancing in the mutual knowledge that they are enjoying themselves. She commented that 'I think that part of the reason why that's important is that there's not a lot of chances you get, there's not a lot of contexts you get, to share things non-verbally with friends.'

At the same time, however, there are elements of the club scene that Kath felt deeply uncomfortable about. One area of particular unease for her is the sexualised nature of clubs: 'A lot of people go to clubs to pull, whereas I actually go because I enjoy dancing . . . I prefer not to make eye contact with other people.' She also expressed discomfort with the use of drugs and the abuse of alcohol that goes on in clubs, and commented negatively on a recent visit to a club in which she had found that some people had passed out drunk early in the evening in the reception area. Kath's way of dealing with the ambivalence that arises for her when she goes clubbing is to separate her positive valuing of dancing from aspects of the club scene that she finds distasteful or harmful. She commented that 'the dancing, to me, is very different to the club culture because it's the dancing that's important to me', and went on to say that 'unfortunately, the only place where you can dance like that is the club.' Kath's experience of clubbing was therefore one of ambivalence in which her valuing of dancing sat in tension with her religious objections to the sexual and drug-related practices of club culture.

Yet another view of clubbing was demonstrated by Paul. He valued clubbing partly because of the intense experiences he had when dancing, but more important to him was the group ethos of the clubs that he goes to. Paul saw this ethos as primarily being friendly and supportive, and commented:

> 'I like the fact that in the sort of clubs that I like going to people help each other out. If someone's not having a good time, people will try and cheer them up even if they don't know them. I've had times when I've lost my friends or whatever, and someone's come over to me and said, "Oh, you don't look like you're having a good time – why don't you come and dance, or whatever." And I like that.'

For Paul, his experiences of clubbing are also characterised by greater freedom in the way that he relates to others. He clearly valued being able to sit down and chat with people that he'd not met before, or to be able to dance with strangers, and for this to be seen as acceptable behaviour. He also talked about how, when he is dancing, he sometimes feels emotionally connected to the people around him and experiences a deep sense of caring for them, even though he does not actually know them. Paul saw these types of experience as generally unique to the kind of clubs that he goes to: 'It's definitely an experience that you can't get any other way, the feeling of being so free and so connected to other people. Certainly you couldn't get it anywhere else really.' Indeed Paul suggested that these kinds of experiences of connecting with others are valuable precisely because they are so rare in normal social interaction. He commented:

> 'For me it says a lot about what I can't get in normal society, things that I can't have. Things like just being able to sit down next to a person and talk to them. Because you just can't do that. If you walked into a pub and sat down at a table with people you didn't know, then they'd just all look at you . . . It's things like that that you can't have and that in some ways I wish you could.'

One reason why Paul believed that the clubs he went to were more friendly and allowed more open social contact was that people did not generally go to these clubs with the primary intention of picking up sexual partners. He made a strong contrast between the kind of clubs he went to and other clubs where people did go primarily to 'pull', with the latter kind of club being a more hostile environment. The fact that people in the clubs that he went to weren't 'on the pull' meant that they felt freer in approaching strangers without this having connotations of trying to 'pick them up'. He observed that:

> 'Just the fact that no one there is trying to pull people just takes so much pressure off everyone. You just go out and have a good time. If you look at someone and you'd quite like to dance with them, then you dance with them and there's nothing more than that to it.'

Another reason why Paul believed the clubs he went to had this special ethos was because they were clubs in which people either took Ecstasy or were sympathetic to the social environment that Ecstasy use can create. Again, he drew contrasts between clubs that he enjoyed going to and others where people would primarily be drinking alcohol or smoking cannabis.

Paul therefore valued going clubbing because through it he was able to experience a particular kind of social environment characterised by friendliness and openness. Within this environment, normal social conventions about contact with strangers, and typical social assumptions about sexual motivations for approaching strangers, were suspended. He was therefore able to experience freedom and a degree of intimacy with people that he had not met before, and this provided him with something that he found his normal day-to-day social interactions did not offer.

The contrasts in the ways in which Louise, Kath and Paul made sense of their clubbing experiences, and in what they valued in those experiences, are striking. Louise values clubbing as a form of entertainment, whereas Kath sees it as a means of experiencing a particular part of her inner self. Kath is highly dubious about many of the practices of club culture and does not discriminate between drug and excessive alcohol use as bad things, whereas Paul sees the ethos of the clubs that he goes to as very positive and believes that Ecstasy use makes a constructive contribution to that. Louise enjoys the sexualised atmosphere of clubs, whereas Kath feels very uncomfortable about it because of her religious beliefs, and Paul actively seeks clubs that are not highly sexualised because he believes they allow greater freedom in social interaction. Paul sees certain aspects of club culture as offering a critique and response to instrumental and superficial social relationships, whereas Louise would not regard clubbing as offering that social critique and Kath would be sceptical about club culture having much that is useful to say about how we should live our lives.

Louise, Kath and Paul all value their clubbing experiences, but the ways in which they interpret these experiences and what they value within them are quite diverse. There is no evidence here of a common 'clubbing spirituality' which provides a shared system of values and meanings for them. Rather, although clubbing is an important part of their lives and is a meaningful and valuable activity for each of them, the way in which they make sense of their clubbing experiences reflects the range of different values and beliefs that they hold.

Popular culture and meaning in a 'post-religious' culture?

This discussion of clubbers' experiences (and the way they make sense of those experiences) illustrates and extends the key ideas that we explored in the previous chapter. Firstly, club culture does seem to be an important resource for some people as they seek to live meaningful lives. Whether it is Valerie's experience of deeper connection with herself, Kath's ability to express an essential non-verbal part of who she is, or Paul's enjoyment of freer and more intimate relationships with others, it is clear that many of the individuals discussed here find something meaningful and valuable in clubbing. Tom Beaudoin's idea that popular culture has an important role to play in the 'Generation X' pursuit of meaning is therefore supported by the experiences of the individual clubbers that we have explored.

However, as we have already seen in the previous chapter, we cannot afford to make simplistic assumptions about the ways in which people will find meaning through popular culture. Just as people will interpret and make use of a film like *The Matrix* in radically different ways, so we have seen here that that this is also true for club culture. What is common amongst the clubbers whose views we have discussed here is that clubbing represents a valuable part of their lives, but the specific meaning and value that clubbing has is different for each of them as individuals. Popular culture does not therefore offer some kind of monolithic set of values and beliefs that people simply passively and uniformly accept. Rather forms of popular culture like clubbing are rich and complex resources that people use in different ways that are personally meaningful for them.

A new issue that has emerged from this chapter concerns the role of 'religious' language in the contemporary search for meaning. Now clearly, for some of these clubbers, their clubbing experiences have at times offered them a profoundly transformed sense of themselves and others. As we saw earlier, other writers such as Malbon and Saunders have also drawn attention to the potentially meditative or mystical quality of clubbing experiences. What is very striking, however, is that these profound experiences rarely seem to be interpreted by clubbers as having some kind of 'religious' significance. Beth provided us with an excellent example of someone to whom it simply did not occur to interpret her clubbing experiences in religious terms. This raises the possibility that for increasing numbers of people in Western culture, the personal pursuit of meaning may be understood and expressed through language, images and concepts that have little connection to 'formal' religion. In this sense, Western culture could then be seen as becoming increasingly 'post-religious', with the individual search for meaning taking on new and surprising forms that are detached from traditional religious ideas and the institutions that continue to maintain them.

There is a growing recognition within the Church that this may indeed be the case, with one very senior Catholic figure referring to Christianity as having been 'largely vanquished' in Western society (news.bbc, 2001). If our society is becoming increasingly 'post-religious', then this is a profoundly important cultural shift. A number of questions arise out of this. What kind of (popular cultural) resources are helping people to make sense of life or find value in it? How can we help people to become more aware or self-critical of the values and beliefs that are important to them? What understandings of life or 'images of God' might be useful for a 'Generation X' pursuit of meaning? Does theology have any useful role to play in helping people think about the meaning of existence, or is it too closely connected to traditional religious ideas to be of any interest or value to the new and emerging ways in which people are pursuing meaning? Can the Church have any kind of constructive role in helping the contemporary search for meaning, or will it now be consigned to helping maintain and minister to the religious life of an ever-diminishing group of people?

Much of this book so far has been concerned with trying to analyse what is happening in terms of the contemporary search for meaning in Western culture. In the final part of this book, though, we will now turn our attention to some of these more 'theological' questions that arise out of our analysis and examine resources that might be useful for the development of a 'Generation X' spirituality and theology.

6

Surprising Moments of Grace: Douglas Coupland and a 'Generation X' Spirituality

Back at the beginning of chapter 2, I mentioned how reading Douglas Coupland's novel *Generation X* was an important experience for me. In his apparently rather directionless account of three young people trying to carve out some meaning in life for themselves, I could see something of my own desire for and struggle to achieve this sense of meaning. From conversations that I have had both with people who have some kind of religious faith or those who do not, it is clear to me that Coupland's work has struck an important chord with others as well. In fact, one researcher looking at emerging trends in the Christian Church said to me that young people he had met as part of his research were more likely to cite Coupland's novels as important influences for them than the writing of any traditional or mainstream Christian theologian.

So far in this book, I have tried to return to what Coupland originally meant by the term 'Generation X', and to see how this attitude of wanting and struggling to find meaning in the contemporary world might be finding expression both within and beyond traditional religious environments. In this chapter, I want to say something more about Coupland's understanding of the difficulty of finding meaning in contemporary culture and then go a stage further in order to try to identify ideas within his work that suggest what kind of meaning we might be able to find in life. Although I am not sure Coupland himself would precisely welcome this kind of language, I am going to try to explore his work to see what he might have to say about the possible forms a 'Generation X spirituality' might take.

Some readers may find my approach in this chapter a little unusual as a style of academic writing. One person, reviewing similar work I have written on Coupland, commented that I seemed to be doing neither theology nor literary criticism, but that I was 'thinking aloud'. I don't think that observation was meant as a compliment at the time, but it probably does suggest that what follows does not neatly fit into academic boxes. It might be fairest to describe the following as a 'meditation' on the meaning of Coupland's work for me, and this may help to explain why I continually slip from making observations about Coupland's texts to observations about our contemporary search for meaning and back again. The following is offered, then, not as an authoritative literary critical analysis of Coupland's work but as a set of personal reflections on how his novels might help those of us with a 'Generation X' view of the world in our own pursuit of meaning.

I went to the desert and there was nothing there: Coupland on the struggle to find meaning

A recurring theme in Douglas Coupland's writing is the sheer difficulty of finding meaning in a world in which, now that traditional religious ideas seem to have lost their power. In Coupland's novel *Life After God*, as he drives through the desert, the narrator finds himself listening to religious radio stations, and the following train of thought develops for him:

> The stations talked about Jesus and salvation and I found it was pretty hard listening because these religious types are always so whacked out and extreme. I think they take things too literally and miss too many points because of this literalism. This has always been the basic flaw with religion – or so I had been taught, and so (I realized) I had come to believe. So at least I knew *one* thing for sure that I believed in.

The radio stations all seemed to be talking about Jesus nonstop, and it seemed to be this crazy orgy of projection, with everyone projecting onto Jesus the antidotes to the things that had gone wrong in their own lives. He is Love. He is Forgiveness. He is Compassion. He is a Wise Career Decision. He is a Child Who Loves Me.

I was feeling a sense of loss as I heard these people. I felt like Jesus was sex – or rather, I felt like I was from another world where sex did not exist and I arrived on Earth and everyone talked about how good sex felt, and showed me their pornography and built their lives around sex, and yet I was forever cut off from the true sexual experience. I did not deny that the existence of Jesus was real to these people – it was merely that I was cut off from their experience in a way that was never connectable. (Coupland, 1994, pp. 182–4)

This extract captures well this sense of disconnection from traditional religious meaning. The narrator here finds that he is no more capable of engaging meaningfully with these religious images than he is able to fly. Rather he finds himself struggling to identify what exactly it is that he does believe, and seems relieved to discover at least a conviction that an approach to life based on a rigid and literal religious dogma is limiting and unproductive.

This extract from *Life After God* is interesting, though, not only for the attitudes that it illustrates but because this train of thought takes place whilst the narrator is travelling through the desert. In many religious traditions the desert holds a special significance as the place to which people can retreat to find meaning or meet with God. It is in the desert that Moses encounters God in the burning bush, and the foundations for Jesus' ministry are laid in his retreat into the wilderness to pray for forty days and nights. Similarly the Christian monastic movement originated with those men and women who left the towns and cities of Roman society to go into the wilderness to pray.

Reflecting this religious notion of the desert retreat, Coupland's novels contain a recurring motif of the individual who chooses to drop out of mainstream urban culture (often to travel through wilderness locations) in order to try to find some meaning in life.

A trip through the desert forms a central part of the narrator's reflections about meaning in *Life After God*. Andy, Dag and Claire, in *Generation X*, move to live on the edge of the Californian desert in their search for meaning. Linus, in *Girlfriend in a Coma*, spends four years wandering the United States in the hope of finding some other meaning to the mundane life he sees stretching ahead of him. Similarly, John Johnson, in *Miss Wyoming*, decides to give up his career, home and possessions to wander across America. He explains this decision as an attempt to 'jimmy myself open and take whatever creature that's sitting inside and shake it clean like a rug and then rinse it in a cold, clear lake like up in Oregon, and then I want to put it under the sun to let it heal and dry and grow and sit and come to consciousness again with a clear and quiet mind' (Coupland, 2000, p. 47).

For many of Coupland's characters, then, the retreat from mainstream urban life to a period of wandering, often through wilderness landscapes, becomes an attempt to find some fresh connection with themselves and with the wider meaning of life. As striking as the recurrent desire for such retreat amongst Coupland's characters, is the fact that it rarely seems to yield any substantial revelations about life's meaning. Andy, Dag and Claire reach no big answers about life, but can glimpse meaning through the stories that they tell each other. Linus and John Johnson both return from their wandering without any much clearer sense about the purpose of life. The narrator of *Life After God* has a chance encounter with a homeless man in the desert who helpfully directs him to the nearest town, and this small act of kindness offers him a fragment of hope that something meaningful and valuable can be experienced in life. But in the desert Coupland's characters encounter no burning bush or voice of God that is able to give them some clear and authoritative view of life. At best, these desert wanderings offer fragments of hope and meaning.

In the absence of meaning from traditional religious ideas, consumer culture or even the wilderness retreat, Coupland's characters find themselves trying to build their own personal sense of purpose in life. Underlying this search for personal meaning is the ongoing threat of disappointment and despair, as the stories and frameworks of meaning that they build for themselves threaten to fall apart in the face of life's realities.[1] In *Life After God*, Coupland touches on this theme in a series of animal stories that the narrator of the book tells to his child. One of these stories concerns 'Squirrelly the Squirrel' who planned to have an exhibition of nut paintings at the Vancouver Art Gallery, but who never managed to do this because he had to get a job in the peanut butter factory when Mrs Squirrelly got pregnant. Another is about 'Clappy the Kitten' who planned to be a movie star, but then ran up too many bills on her MasterCard and had to get a job in a bank. After a while she was too old to become a movie star, or had lost her ambition, and found it easier simply to talk about her dream rather than do anything about it. The narrator reflects on these stories as being about 'beautiful little creatures who were all supposed to have been part of a fairy tale but who got lost along the way' (Coupland, 1994, p. 24).

Within Coupland's work, there is a poignant sense of the disappointment and despair that can accompany the breakdown of the projects that we construct for our lives. In seeking to avoid meaningless and despair, Coupland's characters often resort to an ironic approach to life in which the products and fashions of popular culture, in particular, are treated in a playful way as a reference point for life.[2] Ironic reference to popular culture thus represents a tool for getting through life in a culture without clear meaning, but where there need to be some reference points to which we can relate our lives or which can help us communicate with other people. Coupland is clear, though, about the dangers of irony leading to a disengaged attitude to life. Being ironic may help us to keep a critical and sceptical distance to our culture, but it can also represent a barrier to becoming committed to particular ideas and projects. It may help us to remain 'cool' and culturally credible, but in Coupland's view it can ultimately impede what is most essential about our existence – the committed, personal pursuit of truth and meaning. These themes emerge clearly in the following quote from *Life After God*, in which the narrator reviews his suburban childhood existence and comments:

Life was charmed but without politics or religion. It was the life of the children of the children of the pioneers – life after God – a life of earthly salvation on the edge of heaven. Perhaps this is the finest thing to which we may aspire, the life of peace, the blurring between dream life and real life – and yet I find myself speaking these words with a sense of doubt. I think there was a trade-off somewhere along the line. I think the price we paid for our golden life was an inability to believe in love; instead we gained an irony that scorched everything it touched. And I wonder if this irony is the price we paid for the loss of God. But then I must remind myself we are living creatures – we have religious impulses – we *must* – and yet into what cracks do these impulses flow in a world without religion? It is something I think about every day. Sometimes I think it is the only thing I should be thinking about. (Coupland, 1994, pp. 273f.)

Coupland's novels therefore depict a world in which our search for meaning is a hard and difficult one. He portrays his characters as caught between the consumer lifestyle of urban culture in which the ironic use of popular culture seems the only way of expressing meaning, and retreat beyond urban consumerism to a wilderness that does not yield substantial revelations about life's meaning either. In the midst of this dilemma, his characters (and we ourselves) find ourselves attempting to construct projects that will give our individual lives some meaning, but are prone to despair or mind-numbing addictions when these projects collapse or fail to materialise. Such despair may be avoided through an ironic approach to life, but ultimately even this irony does not really protect us but simply leaves us feeling more profoundly disconnected from life's meaning.

If we (and Coupland) were to stop at this point, then our prospects for living with a sense of purpose in life would seem pretty bleak. Coupland, however, whilst clearly portraying the struggle to find meaning in contemporary society, also offers hope that in the midst of this struggle we can find fragments of meaning that can be enough to help us go on living with a sense of value and purpose. It is to these fragments of hope in his work that we will now turn.

Finding threads for a 'Generation X' spirituality

Whilst Coupland is clear in his novels about the difficulty in finding meaning in life in the contemporary world, he is also equally clear about the importance of not giving up on the search for meaning. This point is strikingly made in his novel *Girlfriend in a Coma*, in which the story is concerned with a group of friends who mysteriously survive a catastrophe that kills the rest of the world's population. A key issue in this story becomes the failure of this group of friends to ask questions about the meaning of life in the face of this catastrophe – why it happened, what it teaches them about the purpose of life. Ultimately it falls to the group's guardian angel, Jared, to challenge and inspire them to search for the meaning of existence. Jared promises to return the group to the time before the cataclysm. Then, in a speech reminiscent of the Great Commission in Matthew's Gospel, he sends them out on this quest:

> '[I]n your new lives you'll have to live entirely for that one sensation – that of imminent truth. And you're going to have to holler for it, steal for it, beg for it – and you're never going to stop asking questions about it twenty-four hours a day, the rest of your life . . . Every day for the rest of your lives, all of your living moments are to be spent making others aware of this need – the need to probe and drill and examine and locate the words that take us to beyond ourselves . . . Ask questions, no, *screech* questions out loud – while kneeling in front of the electric doors at Safeway, demanding other citizens ask questions along with you – while chewing up old textbooks and spitting the words onto downtown sidewalks – outside the Planet Hollywood, outside the stock exchange and outside the Gap . . . Grind questions onto the glass on photocopiers. Scrape challenges onto old auto parts and throw them off of bridges so that future people digging in the mud will question the world, too . . . Make bar codes print out fables, not prices. You can't even throw away a piece of litter unless it has a question

stamped on it – a demand for people to reach a finer place . . .
Ask whatever challenges dead and thoughtless beliefs.'
(Coupland, 1998, pp. 268–9)

Far from abandoning the search for meaning, then, this speech
places it as a basic element of what it means to be human. Whilst
Coupland's work clearly depicts the difficulty in achieving any
final sense of the meaning of life, his novels also emphasise the
importance of remaining open to the possibility that we may
encounter meaning and truth, even if in surprising ways and
places.

The meanings that we do encounter may be fragmentary, but
can still offer some basis of hope for our lives. Recalling the
kindness of the homeless drifter in the desert, the narrator in *Life
After God* comments:

> How often is it we are rescued by a stranger, if ever at all?
> And how is it that our lives can become drained of the
> possibility of forgiveness and kindness – so drained that
> even one small act of mercy becomes a potent life-long
> memory? How do our lives reach these points? It is with
> these thoughts in mind that I now see the drifter's wind-
> burned face when I now consider my world – his face
> reminds me that there is still something left to believe in
> after there is nothing left to believe in. (Coupland, 1994,
> pp. 212–3)

These fragments of hope and meaning may come to us in ways
that we do not expect, and certainly in ways that we cannot
control. Whether it is in receiving a spontaneous hug from a
group of children with learning disabilities (as at the end of
Generation X), seeing a dust storm caught in rain and sunshine
(as at the end of *Miss Wyoming*) or the sensation of floating in
an ice-cold mountain pool (as at the end of *Life After God*), brief,
unexpected experiences can act as small signs of life's meaning.
These truncated experiences do not provide us with a grand
theory or philosophy of life, but they provide us with specific
insights such as that kindness is possible, that the struggle of our
lives can have a certain beauty to it, or that we are fundamentally
acceptable and accepted.

Two particular points can be made about the kind of fragmentary experiences of meaning that Coupland narrates in his novels. Firstly, although he does not directly use the word himself, these experiences reflect the theological notion of 'grace'. They are experiences of grace in the sense that they are given to us, they come from beyond us, they are not under our control. Coupland's characters do not have their most meaningful experiences by constructing elaborate philosophies of life. Rather, as in the examples just given of the hug, the sight of the dust storm or the sensation of the freezing pool, they encounter meaning through the acts of others or through particular experiences of the natural world. These fragmentary experiences of meaning are not therefore things to be captured or created, but are things that are given to us in ways, times and places that are beyond our control. Rather than the bleak post-modern or existentialist idea that we live in a world that is meaningless and in which we are left to create our own meaning, Coupland thus depicts a world in which there is meaning that we can encounter. This is meaning that we occasionally glimpse if we can remain open to signs of kindness, beauty and care around us.

One implication of these 'gracious' experiences of meaning is that we cannot make assumptions about where goodness, kindness and healing are necessarily to be found. Within Coupland's work, then, there is often a sense of pragmatism in which things and people are judged not by their superficial social value or their adherence to conventional social norms, but by whether they are genuinely sources of meaning, value and healing. Thus the narrator in *Life After God*, whilst unable to find meaning in religious broadcasts, recognises that the people talking about Jesus on the radio have experienced something valuable for themselves:

> And yet I had to ask myself over and over what it was that these radio people were seeing in the face of Jesus. They sounded like their lives had once been so messed up and lost as they spoke; at least they were no longer so lost anymore – like AA people. So I figured that was a good thing. (Coupland, 1994, pp. 183–4)

Similarly, mediators of kindness and care in Coupland's novels can often be unexpected figures – Wade, the family member in *All Families are Psychotic* with a criminal record, the homeless drifter in *Life After God* or the learning disabled youngsters in *Generation X*. The idea that meaning comes to us, graciously, in unexpected and uncontrolled ways thus leads us away from approaching life on the basis of a particular rigid system of dogma, or moral or social code, to a more open attitude of being ready to encounter signs of meaning wherever they may be found.

A second point to be made about these fragmentary experiences of meaning that Coupland describes is that they often involve physical experience. Rather than meaning being discovered through abstract thought, Coupland's characters have experiences of meaning mediated to them through touch, sight and sound. In contrast to philosophical or theological traditions that have emphasised the importance of abstract, rational thought in the pursuit of truth, Coupland's notion of meaning is very much one that is *embodied*. This is well illustrated by the closing lines of *Life After God*:

> I peel my clothes and step into the pool beside the burbling stream, onto polished rocks, and water so clear that it seems it might not even be really there . . . And the water from the stream above me roars. Oh, does it roar! Like a voice that knows only one message, one truth – never-ending, like the clapping of hands and the cheers of the citizens upon the coronation of the king, the crowds of the inauguration, cheering for hope and for that one voice that will speak to them . . .
>
> I walk deeper and deeper into the rushing water. My testicles pull up into myself. The water enters my belly button and it freezes my chest, my arms and my neck. It reaches my mouth, my nose, my ears and the roar is so loud – this roar, this clapping of hands. These hands – the hands that heal; the hands that hold; the hands we desire because they are better than desire.
>
> I submerge myself in the pool completely. I grab my knees and I forget gravity and I float within the pool and yet, even here, I hear the roar of water, the roar of clapping hands.

These hands – the hands that care, the hands that mold; the
hands that touch the lips, the lips that speak the words –
the words that tell us we are whole. (Coupland, 1994,
pp. 357–60)

In the same way that mystical writers have often reported a
strong physical element to their experiences of divine revelation
(see, e.g., Wiethaus, 1996), so the experiences of meaning that
Coupland describes are bound up with physical sensation.
Meaning is found, then, not through 'pure' mental or spiritual
activity, but through our physical experience of other people and
the world around us.

In his novels, then, Douglas Coupland depicts the search for
meaning in the contemporary world as a difficult one. But he
does not present our existence as one that is wholly without
meaning. Rather, he presents meaning as something that can
come to us in glimpses, through isolated, fragmented experiences
in which for a moment we gain a sense that life is valuable, that
kindness is possible, that we can be accepted. In this sense, the
phrase 'the search for meaning' that I have used throughout this
book may actually be a less helpful way of thinking about
this process. Rather than us searching for meaning, meaning
ultimately comes to us or finds us. The notion of the 'search' for
meaning remains appropriate, though, in the sense that we still
need to maintain an open attitude in which we are ready to
receive these fragmented signs of meaning when they appear
to us.

Coupland's notion of meaning coming to us through these
fragmented experiences is striking in the wider context of the
discussion we have engaged in from the start of the book. One
of the key recurring themes in this discussion has been the
idea that the 'Generation X' search for meaning is one in which
individuals try to establish a sense of meaning and value in life
that feels personally authentic to them. In chapter 2, we understood that this desire for personally authentic meaning was an
important part of the lives of many of the characters of Coupland's novels. In chapter 3, we saw how this desire for personally
authentic meaning was leading some individuals and groups to
move towards a more critical view of traditional Evangelical

Christian ideas and beliefs and innovative new ways of engaging in religious worship. Similarly, in chapters 4 and 5, we noted how people may make use of popular culture to express what is meaningful and valuable in life – but that they are likely to do this in ways that are personally meaningful to them rather than in a way that is dictated by popular culture itself.

This emphasis on personal authenticity in the contemporary search for meaning could lead us to conclude that it is purely for us to define the meaning of life, that truth is what we make it. But this discussion of Coupland's work has raised an alternative notion – that meaning comes to us through experiences that are beyond our control, through moments of grace in which we catch a glimpse of a reality beyond our individual choices, aspirations and failings. We are thus faced with another alternative beyond the pre-packaged truths of political, religious or corporate organisations and the individual projects we choose to construct for our own lives – the possibility of a greater reality that we might glimpse fleetingly at different points through our lives.

If we accept this idea that emerges from Coupland's work, then this may have fundamental implications for the way in which we think about life and decide to live it. Rather than being an exercise in simply marking time in as pleasurable or interesting ways as we can before we die, life would then become an attempt to remain open to experiences that help us gain a sense of its meaning and to value these experiences when they come to us. This belief in the possibility of discovering meaning in life cannot be a naïve attitude if it is to be sustainable through our lives. At different times, as individuals, we may be exposed to illness, loneliness, betrayal, disappointment, amongst other experiences, and these may raise basic doubts for us as to whether life can have any meaning. Furthermore, the experience of living in a society where we may feel alienated from its institutions or from the superficiality of consumer culture, may deepen our struggle to achieve a sense of meaning in life. Nevertheless, the 'Generation X' search for meaning is ultimately faced with the question of whether there is a meaning that lies beyond us or whether (like Scheherazade in the *Tales of the Arabian Nights*) we are simply creating stories for ourselves to keep us going until we die.

Coupland's fiction offers the possibility that we may discover some meaning beyond ourselves, even if our glimpses of it are only partial and fleeting. This inevitably raises further questions about how we might understand ultimate reality, and whether the notion of 'God' has any useful part to play in this. It is to these questions that we will now turn in the final chapter.

7
Does 'Generation X' Need 'God'?

When I was at college, I used to keep a kind of spiritual journal in which I would record my thoughts about what was going on in my life and any particular prayers I wanted to make at that time. When I look back at that journal now I can see that 'God' was a formidable presence in my life. I clearly felt that all of my energies should be devoted to pleasing God, that anything good in my life was a sign of God's love for me and that my life was an ongoing struggle of living up to what God hoped and expected from me. For a long period of time I also believed that God was actively involved in the world, and that if people loved him and prayed to him enough then he would see them through and things would turn out all right in the end.

This deep belief in a personal, active God began to disintegrate over a number of years, however. As I began to develop greater self-esteem, I found that there was less need in my psyche for a God who made me feel good because I was part of his plans. As I began to become more mature and take more responsibility for my life, I began to realise that my desire to be guided by God had often previously hidden a fear on my part of taking my own decisions. As I became more aware of the depth and persistence of people's suffering in the world, I found I could no longer maintain a belief in a God who would apparently intervene in the world to help a church raise money for its building projects whilst standing by and permitting terrible and degrading experiences of sickness, poverty, abuse and violence. The 'God' who had been such a central part of that spiritual journal gradually evaporated out of my life like a fading morning mist.

Again this experience of losing a particular set of beliefs about God (and struggling to find some new ones) has made me aware of the wider question of what role, if any, 'God' has to play in the contemporary search for meaning. Does a healthy spirituality need to find some place for 'God' in it, and what concepts of 'God' are better, or more true to our experience, than others? Does the 'Generation X' search for meaning need 'God'?

Western culture (despite the numerical decline of those involved in formal religion) seems to be highly ambivalent on this issue. On the one hand, we can see images and ideas within popular culture that suggest that 'God' has at best a marginal significance for many people today. The claim that 'God is a DJ' is not so much a statement about God's skill on the decks, as an indication that meaning might be found in life in places beyond a belief in a transcendent, divine being. Similarly, the TV programme *South Park* represents Jesus as the host of a poor quality cable TV chat show with a tiny audience that rarely reaches double figures. Despite the sense in *South Park* that Jesus may be one of the few people trying to live with some kind of moral integrity, it is clear that he is a marginal figure who has little power to inspire or interest people any more.

On the other hand, interest in 'God' still seems very much a part of Western culture. A recent non-fiction bestseller in Britain and the United States has been Neale Donald Walsch's series of books *Conversations with God* (see, e.g., Walsch, 1997), in which the central premise is that the author is engaged in an exchange of letters with God about the meaning of life. Popular TV programmes such as *The Simpsons* and *God, the Devil and Bob* also retain the notion of an omnipotent, transcendent God, which suggests that it is still more interesting and engaging (at least within the perspectives of these programmes) to tell stories about the world in which 'God' is present.

In this final chapter, I want briefly to explore three different views on the usefulness and importance of 'God' for the contemporary search for meaning. Discussing these will help us to focus on some of the issues that are involved in the decision to see 'God' as crucial or passé in our contemporary attempts to find some meaning and value in life.

Beyond a consumer spirituality

'Spirituality is on sale at a High Street and shopping mall near you' (Starkey, 1997, p. 113). 'Spirituality' has been a huge growth industry over the past decade. Despite the fact that we lack clear and commonly agreed definitions of what 'spirituality' actually is, sales of spirituality 'products' such as books in the 'Mind, Body, Spirit' sections of bookstores, workshops and consultations on meditation or other 'spiritual' practices, or CDs of 'spiritual' music from different parts of the world, have flourished. 'Spirituality' is touching not only our purchasing habits, but wider cultural notions of health as well, with an increasing awareness evident both in health-care and psychotherapy of the importance of working constructively with patients' or clients' personal spiritualities.

The way in which the term 'spirituality' seems to be most commonly used in contemporary culture is as a kind of signpost that indicates that people have a need to live with a sense of meaning, value and mystery. It therefore tends to be identified with anything that can help someone attain that sense of meaning and value, or to feel 'spiritual' in relation to their life. The British Christian writer Mike Starkey has suggested that this inclusive notion of spirituality as being whatever helps people find meaning is both a fitting one for our culture and also a deeply problematic one:

> [L]et us imagine the children of the post-war consumer boom in search of religion. They are a culture raised on an unparalleled choice of foods from around the world, an unprecedented range of media options, a vast choice of clothing, furnishings, reading-matter and leisure pursuits. For such people the one non-negotiable is that they stand at the centre of their own universe, able to select the goods, people and experiences they choose. Such a culture goes off in search of religion and comes up with 'spirituality' . . . It is a religion where the self is at the centre, where all the faiths and myths of history are trawled in the search for

happy inner experiences, where nobody or nothing impedes freedom of choice. It is spirituality as lifestyle accessory . . .

But for all the use of vogue terms such as 'deep', 'profound', 'inner' and 'mystery', such a spirituality is appallingly shallow. Not only does it fail to challenge the complacency of Western consumer capitalism, it is a product of it. Not only does it fail to challenge personal selfishness, it is its religious expression. Such is the religious illiteracy of our culture that we fail to spot that such 'spirituality' is no solution. We live in an age which can tell the difference between Coke and Pepsi, but not between good religion and bad religion. Consumer spirituality, far from being the answer, is simply a restatement of the problem using mystical jargon. (Starkey, 1997, pp. 119, 121)

Starkey is clear, then, that the contemporary interest in 'spirituality' is an expression of a culture in which we are used to acting, and thinking of ourselves, as consumers. Far from indicating a connection with profound religious or spiritual truths, Starkey suggests that such consumer spirituality is inherently superficial and reflects a pursuit of what makes us feel good rather than what is true. From our discussion previously in chapters 4 and 5, we can see that there is at least some merit in Starkey's analysis. In those earlier chapters we saw how individuals can interpret and make use of popular culture in distinctive and idiosyncratic ways as they try to express what is important in life to them. The different ways in which people responded to *The Matrix* or to club culture reflected their own personal beliefs and concerns, and these responses can be seen as clear choices by these individuals in terms of how they wanted to express themselves or their beliefs in life. In this sense, then, it is possible to see these individuals as 'consumers' of popular culture, choosing which parts of that culture to engage with and then using those cultural forms to express themselves and their beliefs. In the same way, Starkey suggests that much contemporary spirituality consists of a 'consumption' of religion, in which consumers sift through religious images, ideas and practices in much the way that one would look through different clothes-racks in a fashion store, choosing those items that one finds interesting or congenial and discarding the rest.

For some readers, the idea of spirituality as a consumer approach to religion may not make it any less attractive. After all, this approach seems to place a high value on individual expression, freedom, choice and creativity, which could all be argued to be good things. What Starkey is critical of, however, is precisely the fundamental importance that is given to individual choice in this approach. His basic argument here is that it is wholly narcissistic for us to imagine that it is purely up to our own individual choice and imagination to define what the true meaning of life is. Indeed, Starkey suggests, unless we are prepared to retain the narcissistic fantasy that it is we ourselves as individuals who give life its meaning, then we need to engage with the God who is beyond us and who is the source of all meaning. So ingrained is our consumer approach to religion, that Starkey argues the notion of a God who is truly over and beyond us – and that our lives are created by God rather than by ourselves – can actually come as a shock to us. Despite the potentially alien nature of this concept to a consumer psyche, however, Starkey proposes that it is only this real, external God who can give us a fixed and stable meaning to our lives. He contrasts this faith in God with a consumer spirituality, commenting:

> Generation X asks 'Who am I?' The shopping mall say: 'You are a consumer; buy an identity.' The humanist says: 'You are an individual; sort yourself out.' The bestselling writer on spirituality says: 'You are in need of self-realization; go deeper within.' The Xer replies: 'I have bought so many identities I no longer have a clue who I am. I participate in a culture of selfishness so screwed up that I can do nothing to change my world. I have gone deeper within and found only emptiness. My inheritance is to be a person of no fixed identity in a world with no wonder.'
>
> God says: 'You are a person made in my image. You are made for intimacy with me and with others, to care for my earth and develop its potential. Your inheritance is to have

a stable identity, in a world charged up with glory. Be reborn into wonder.' (Starkey, 1997, p. 126)

If Starkey is right to characterise much of contemporary spirituality as fundamentally narcissistic then this should at least give us pause for thought. Is it credible for us to claim that we are the ultimate arbiters of what is meaningful in life and that there is nothing beyond us that defines what true meaning and value is? Certainly (perhaps for some readers at least) Starkey's idea of this benevolent God who can act as the true and lasting basis for our identity and sense of purpose might offer an attractive alternative to narcissistic consumerism. But what might prevent people from being able to engage with this image of a loving, powerful, creator God who exists over and beyond us in the contemporary search for meaning?

After God: the need for humanism in a world of suffering

In discussing the problem with belief in a personal God, the theologian Anthony Pinn gives a short anecdote from an African-American folktale called 'The Preacher and His Farmer Brother'. In this story, the preacher visits his brother's sugar cane farm after a twenty-year absence and remarks that thanks to God's help his brother has now got a pretty productive farm. His brother replies that the preacher should have seen the farm when God had it just by himself. The clear implication here is that what has been decisive has not been the hand of God on the farm, but the hard work that the farmer has put in to keep his land productive and prevent it from returning to the wild.

This story illustrates a central argument that Pinn puts forward, namely that it is far more credible to understand events in the world in terms of human actions and motivations than in terms of a loving, powerful, personal God who has a hand in directing them. Pinn comments:

> There is no evidence of God's existence (no progress humans cannot easily take credit for and no suffering they are

incapable of fostering), but on the other hand, there is no doubt that humans exist (ironically, moral evil and suffering scream this existence). Strong humanism considers theistic answers to existential questions simplistic and geared toward psychological comfort without respect for the complexity of the human condition. (Pinn, 1995, p. 142)

From this perspective, then, Starkey's emphasis on belief in a powerful, loving, personal God may offer the prospect of psychological comfort, but it also represents a denial or distortion of our real experience of life. Pinn argues that this is particularly the case if we consider the issue of suffering. The attempt to explain both the reality of suffering and the existence of God is hardly a new exercise, and goes back at least to the writing of the Book of Job in the Hebrew Scriptures. Pinn's view, however, is that such attempts to reconcile the presence of suffering in the world and the existence of God inevitably lead to complex theological gymnastics and the production of unsatisfactory explanations. For example, we could say that God allows suffering because he has chosen to limit his power in order to give us free will, and that it is the inappropriate use of our free will that ultimately causes suffering. But if this is the case, Pinn observes, our concern should be with how we use our free will and the question of belief in God becomes a secondary or unimportant issue. Alternatively, we could say that a loving God allows suffering because it has some redemptive quality to it – it can make us better people in some way. As Pinn comments, though, this approach can simply deny the crushing effect that suffering can have upon people and can lead to people passively accepting their suffering as something given by God rather than resisting what may be causing it. Thirdly, we could explain suffering in the world by saying that God has a dark side, and that some of God's actions harm us just as some heal or redeem us. Whilst this seems to take the reality of human suffering more seriously, Pinn notes that this ultimately gives us a picture of a morally ambivalent God for whose existence we still have no real evidence. Ultimately, Pinn concludes, the most reasonable explanation for human suffering that we can yet identify is to understand it purely in terms of human actions – for it is we alone who can act to cause or reduce suffering – and not to attempt to understand suffering with reference to some kind of external God. Indeed, moving beyond belief in God becomes an important basis for beginning to see our own responsibility in addressing suffering:

> In removing even the most covert possibility of divine approval for suffering, strong humanism frees the oppressed to fight for social transformation. The importance of human struggle for change is highlighted and amplified by strong humanism because there are no external sources of assistance. Humanity has complete control over its destiny and therefore one cannot hide behind God and claim that nonaction is a divine command. (Pinn, 1995, p. 157)

Pinn's view of the world has close affinities to the existential philosophy of Jean-Paul Sartre. Sartre claimed that we live in a universe without God, in which there are no absolute laws we should follow or absolute values we should live by. In such a universe without any ultimate or absolute meaning given by God, Sartre (1948) suggested that we are 'condemned to be free' and that we have no real alternative other than to make free choices about how we will live our lives (p. 34). To deny that we are abandoned to this kind of freedom, or to seek solace in unthinkingly following social norms or roles, represents an act of 'bad faith' (see Sartre, 1958, pp. 47ff.). The meaning of life is therefore made out of the ways in which we ourselves choose to live and act. Or in Sartre's own words: 'Life is nothing until it is lived; but it is yours to make sense of, and the value of it is nothing else but the sense that you choose' (1948, p. 54).

Now this idea that there is no God, no absolute meaning, and that we are left alone in the universe to make our own sense out of life, may seem a depressing or nihilistic one. But both Pinn and Sartre would claim that this idea is in fact a liberating and positive one. As Pinn puts it, 'it places human destiny in the hands of humans' (1995, p. 157). We may be alone in the universe but this leaves us with the awesome responsibility to fashion our own lives, and not to fall back into a fantasy of being rescued by 'God' or to retreat into a dream-world of aspirations which we never put into practice through our real actions. To quote the

'Talk Talk' song, 'life's what you make it'. If we can bear the disconcerting weight of this responsibility, we find that we are freed to engage with life in ways that are potentially authentic, creative and constructive. If, in practice, we act in ways that are damaging to others rather than helpful to them, then this is our responsibility and no one else's. We are freed to act in the world as we choose, in the knowledge that it is the actions we take (rather than our claimed beliefs, aspirations or fantasies) that make up the sum of the meaning of our lives.

From this perspective, Starkey's call to faith in a personal, loving God who underwrites our lives represents an infantile longing for protection in the universe from a greater power. By contrast, Pinn and Sartre's perspectives could be depicted as a call for us to take an adult sense of responsibility for ourselves and our lives in the knowledge that there is no greater Parent figure who will protect us or give meaning to us. A difficulty that Starkey identifies with the views advocated by Pinn and Sartre is, however, that this notion of needing to choose the meaning of our lives can precisely lead us into confusion and uncertainty as we struggle to find our way through life without any clear signposts. We noted in the previous chapter that our attempts to construct projects to give meaning to our lives can be fragile and that the 'Generation X' pursuit of meaning can be prone to despair when the projects around which we build our lives collapse or fail to materialise. And it is precisely from the perspective of this despair that we can see why Starkey's idea of a loving, personal God who can give us a sense of stable identity and meaning in life could be attractive.

Starkey's emphasis on the notion of orienting our lives around a personal, powerful and loving God thus seems to have the advantage of giving some clear and fixed point for our lives, and this could be a source of psychological comfort.[1] Yet the personal, loving and powerful God that Starkey invites us to believe in can seem hard to reconcile with our actual experience of the world. Indeed, as Pinn observes, attempts to reconcile the existence of such a God with the reality of suffering in the world are generally unconvincing apart from to those people who are deeply committed to retaining their belief in God. Despite their claims to be optimistic, however, the view of the world offered by writers such as Pinn and Sartre seems rather bleak. If we are left purely alone as individuals to construct our own meaning in life then the benefits of a sense of freedom and responsibility seem to be off-set by the threat of despair in the face of loneliness and meaninglessness. What alternative do we have to these two polarised positions then?

The 'God above God' – Paul Tillich as a theologian for 'Generation X'

I want to suggest here that a promising alternative approach to thinking about 'God' for the contemporary search for meaning can be found in the work of the German theologian, Paul Tillich. Tillich, who died in 1965, was one of the best-known theologians of the twentieth-century, working initially in Germany and then in America when he fled Germany in 1933 in the face of the growth of Nazism. Tillich's life is itself highly interesting as he combined his important public profile as a theologian with an unorthodox private life, including a complex relationship with his wife, Hannah, and a number of extra-marital affairs (May, 1974; Tillich, 1974; Pauck and Pauck, 1976). Tillich himself was deeply conscious of the ambiguities of his life, and referred to himself as carrying a 'bag of demons' in contrast to the 'bag of grace' carried by a Catholic priest friend of his. Yet he remained highly influential on a number of people who either studied under him, or who encountered his ideas through his lectures, sermons or books.

Whilst debates in academic theology have moved on to new topics, and new approaches to theology have flourished since Tillich died, his work remains highly relevant to the contemporary search for meaning as we have described it in this book. Indeed Tillich's fundamental concern in his work with existential themes such as the struggle to find meaning in life, in the face of loneliness, despair and death, suggests that he may have something useful to contribute to a discussion of the 'Generation X' pursuit of meaning.

Part of Tillich's motivation in developing his theological ideas was his sense that, in twentieth-century Western culture, people were becoming increasingly alienated from traditional religious beliefs and practices. Talk about 'God', 'sin' and 'salvation' simply seemed too far removed from many people's experience for it to have any real significance for them. From our discussion in the first couple of chapters in this book we can see that, if anything, the alienation from traditional religious beliefs and practices that Tillich identified has accelerated and grown as the twentieth century has passed into the twenty-first. Tillich recognised that the loss of connection with traditional religious ideas and images could leave people with a significant struggle to understand the meaning of life, and that a growing sense of meaninglessness in life could result in a profound sense of despair. A fundamental conviction for Tillich, however, is that even if we experience life as meaningless, we are not ultimately abandoned to construct our own meaning in an empty universe (as Sartre would suggest). Rather, Tillich claimed, even in the midst of our most profound despair at finding any meaning in life, we are never cut off from ultimate reality or what Tillich called the 'ground of our being'.

When talking about the 'ground of our being', Tillich some-times used the word 'God' to refer to it. But it is clear that Tillich's notion of 'God' here is quite different to the loving, personal God advocated by Starkey and rejected by Pinn. Indeed, when Tillich talked about this ultimate God, he spoke of it as the 'God above God', a reality that transcends and goes beyond any specific image or concept of God that we have (see Tillich, 2000, p. 179). For Tillich, then, the true meaning of the notion 'God' is that there is a greater reality of which we are a part, a greater reality sustaining our individual lives (the 'ground of our being') which we cannot reduce to particular images or concepts. This idea is not original to Tillich, and can be found, for example, in earlier Christian mystics who claimed that ultimate reality transcends all particular concepts of 'God', that we could only think of God in terms of metaphors of pure light or pure dark-ness, and that this 'God' could be approached through silence rather than through words.[2] Tillich's 'God', then, is not the per-sonal, loving, parental figure of popular Christian belief, but the ultimate reality of which we are a part and for which we have no adequate name (Tillich, 2000, p. 179).

Whilst Tillich rejected the simple characterisation of this ultimate reality as a 'personal God', he nevertheless believed that an awareness of this greater reality could have profoundly personal implications for us. Indeed Tillich suggested that this ultimate reality, this 'ground of our being', could be a source of grace to us, breaking into our lives and reassuring us of our value. In a passionate and eloquent part of one of his sermons, Tillich claimed:

> Grace strikes us when we are in great pain and restlessness. It strikes us when we walk through the dark valley of a meaningless and empty life. It strikes us when our disgust for our own being, our indifference, our weakness, our hostility, and our lack of direction and composure have become intolerable to us. It strikes us when, year after year, the longed-for perfection of life does not appear, when the old compulsions reign within us as they have for decades, when despair destroys all joy and courage. Sometimes at that moment a wave of light breaks into our darkness, and it is as though a voice were saying: 'You are accepted. You are accepted, accepted by that which is greater than you, and the name of which you do not know. Do not ask the name now; perhaps you will find it later. Do not try to do anything now; perhaps later you will do much . . . Simply accept the fact that you are accepted!' If that happens to us, we experience grace. After such an experience we may not be better than before, and we may not believe more than before. But everything is transformed . . . And nothing is demanded of this experience, no religious or moral or intellectual presupposition, nothing but acceptance. (Tillich, 1949, pp. 163f.)

Tillich's ideas here bear a close relation to the theme we noted in Douglas Coupland's work of discrete experiences which give us some sense of the meaning and value in life. Tillich describes these experiences as moments when grace comes to us, when we have a fleeting glance of being part of a reality greater than ourselves. As in Coupland's novels, Tillich does not see these experiences as necessarily providing us with a grand philosophy or theology that makes sense of life ('After such an experience . . . we may not believe more than before'). Nevertheless, these experiences are transformative because they provide us with a glimpse of meaning in life that can inspire us to carrying on living in hopeful and creative ways.

It is precisely such moments of encounter with the 'ground of being' that can give us what Tillich describes as the 'courage to be'. This courage is the ability to acknowledge that our lives are limited, that the universe can seem a random and meaningless place, and that our lives will inevitably come to an end one day. Yet – as Tillich put it – we can demonstrate faith and courage if we can still live in constructive and creative ways *in spite of* these realities. Such faith is not something that we can generate purely within ourselves, however, but arises out of our awareness of that which is greater than ourselves and our individual lives. As Tillich (2000, p. 173) put it:

> Faith is not an opinion but a state. It is the state of being grasped by the power of being which transcends everything that is and in which everything that is participates. He [sic] who is grasped by this power is able to affirm himself because he knows that he is affirmed by the power of being-itself.

Faith for Tillich, then, does not therefore consist of a commitment to a particular set of religious doctrines or 'belief in something unbelievable' (ibid., p. 173). Nor does true faith represent an attempt to deny the basic realities of loneliness, despair and death that we may have to face. Rather faith is an experience in which we become aware of a greater context for our lives, a sense of being part of something greater which helps us both to acknowledge honestly the limitations of our lives and yet to carry on living in constructive ways. Faith is the recognition that, even in the midst of despair, we are never fundamentally cut off from the ultimate living reality of the universe. We may struggle to articulate this faith – and we may never find religious symbols or language that are really adequate to express our experience of the greater 'ground of our being' – but this experience of faith can be enough to carry on living courageously even in the absence of grand ideas, beliefs, stories or concepts that help us to make sense of life.

Tillich's approach therefore represents another alternative to those offered by Starkey and Pinn. As we have seen, Starkey sees the best hope for the 'Generation X' search for meaning as being a turn to a personal, loving God who can offer a stable basis for our identities and our approach to life. Pinn, by contrast, sees the best way forward as precisely a rejection of this parental idea of 'God' and a recognition of our own responsibility to find our own meaning in life and to act in ways that promote human well-being. Tillich recognised that for many people the faith in a personal God that Starkey commends is simply not a credible or possible option. Such a notion of 'God' is simply too alien to many people's experience for it to become an organising force for their lives. Yet Tillich did not accept the view of writers such as Pinn and Sartre who depict the universe as an ultimately meaningless and empty place in which we are abandoned to find our own meaning. Rather he maintained that we are always part of something greater than ourselves, and that it is our moments of awareness of this greater 'ground of our being' that can give us the courage to carry on living in the absence of neat or clear answers about life.

And religion?

In this chapter and the previous one, we have made some initial exploration into what form a 'Generation X' spirituality might take, and what notion of 'God' might be useful for this. In bringing this book to a close, it will be useful to draw together some of the threads of this discussion and to reflect on what the implications of this 'Generation X' search for meaning might be for religion. In the book as a whole we have considered the idea that the 'Generation X' search for meaning is one in which individuals are trying to make sense of their lives in a way that feels personally authentic to them rather than simply accepting the pre-packaged truths of religious, political or corporate organisations. In these last two chapters, we have also outlined some more specific forms that this search for meaning might take.

Referring back to Douglas Coupland's writing, we have noted that we might find meaning in our lives not primarily through grand philosophies or theories of life, but through brief, discrete experiences that help us glimpse meaning and value in our lives. We also saw in his work the idea that these experiences are often bound up with our physical, non-verbal experience. In this chapter, we have looked at different perspectives on the usefulness and importance of 'God' for the 'Generation X' pursuit of meaning. In particular, the work of Paul Tillich seems to offer some promising connections with that of Douglas Coupland. Tillich tries to focus our attention on the 'ground of our being', the unnameable ultimate reality of our existence which, at particular times, can break into our lives and give us a brief, but potentially transformative experience of meaning and value. Again this 'God above God' defies categorisation into neat theologies or philosophies of life, but stands as the reassurance that even in our most profound moments of loneliness or meaninglessness we are never cut off from a reality greater than our individual lives.

In this last part of the book, I want to speculate briefly on some of the implications of Coupland's and Tillich's ideas here for the future of religion in Western culture. If we imagine that we are more likely to achieve meaning in our lives by being open to experiences (often physical and non-verbal) that give us a sense of being part of a greater reality, then what forms of 'religion' are most likely to help us in this? It seems clear that religious forms that are least likely to be helpful are those which try to co-opt us into a schematised and dogmatic view of the world based on predetermined religious doctrines. Religious fundamentalism may have a number of positive effects for its adherents, such as maintaining a sense of personal and communal identity, giving a clear model for moral action in the world, and possibly giving a sense of hope that what is wrong in the world may one day be put right by divine action. What religious fundamentalism seems very poor at, however, is in allowing the kind of attitude to life that Coupland presents in his novels, one of being open to finding meaning in one's experiences in fragmented, personal ways and from surprising sources. Religious fundamentalism will tend to emphasise that truth is attained through adherence to a particular religious text or set of doctrines. Coupland is inviting us to be open to how our lived, physical experience can give us a glimpse of greater meaning. Religious fundamentalism will tend to emphasise that 'God', the truth, or at least 'God's will', is knowable. Tillich points us to a 'God above God', the ultimate reality that lies beyond any concept or label we can create, of which we may be fleetingly aware at different points in our lives.

So if religious fundamentalism is unhelpful to the kind of search for meaning that Coupland and Tillich describe, what 'religious' forms might be more useful? If openness to significant physical, non-verbal experiences are an important element in the pursuit of meaningful life, then we can begin to see that helpful 'religion' in contemporary culture may take a much wider variety of forms than the institutional religion found in churches, synagogues and mosques. Arguably, one of the striking features of contemporary Western culture is the emphasis on activities that are focused around physical or non-verbal experience. These take a wide variety of forms from more overtly 'spiritual' activities such as meditation or yoga, through outdoor activities such as walking, travel to remote parts of the world and playing sport, through to other forms of popular culture such as dance. Recent years have also seen the growth of adrenaline-stimulating sports such as sky-diving, white-water rafting and bungee-jumping, as well as other sports such as skateboarding, surfing and snowboarding which have developed their own particular sub-culture. For me personally, some of the most significant moments in my past year have been spent with groups in which we were performing Latin or African drumming together. Now it is clearly easy enough to depict all of these as simply leisure activities, or perhaps to characterise them as expressions of hedonism in contemporary culture and to say that people engage in them simply because they find them pleasurable. But if, even if just very rarely, we gain a sense of connection with a greater reality or a sense of indescribable joy or deep peace of mind through these physical activities then they could be seen as contributing to a search for meaning that goes beyond pure hedonism.

Whilst there is scope for studying these cultural phenomena in more depth, there is at least some initial evidence to suggest that this range of physical activities can constitute a source of meaning in individuals' lives. In chapter 5 we noted Ben Malbon's idea that many clubbers have 'oceanic' experiences whilst dancing in which they feel part of a greater reality than their individual selves. Douglas Rushkoff (1999) has also, for example, drawn attention to the significant sense of connection with a greater natural order that some surfers claim to experience through their sport. It may well be, then, that declining church attendance in Western societies does not necessarily indicate that Western culture is simply lapsing into mindless hedonism. Rather it may suggest (at least in part) that many individuals recognise that they are more likely to have significant, personally meaningful experiences through a range of physical activities than through associating themselves with a traditional set of religious doctrines or rituals (see, e.g., Amoda, 2001). In making this claim, I am not particularly wanting to suggest that all of the popular cultural activities that I have just described could be seen as 'religions'. In the face of declining church attendance, there has been something of a trend to identify new 'surrogate' religions that are taking their place. We saw, in chapter 5, some of the claims that clubbing can function as such a surrogate religion, and similar claims have, for example, been made about the religious nature of football fandom (Percy and Taylor, 1997). In practice, I think that the idea of 'x' (insert your own preferred popular cultural phenomena, e.g. football, shopping at IKEA, cooking) as a religion generally leads to rather laboured analogies about the ritual significance of cheering a goal or buying pine shelving. Nevertheless the kind of physical activities mentioned above may have a 'religious' element for some people if they offer them an occasional experience of something greater than their individual lives that can give them a sense of peace, meaning, joy or value. Talking more about these occasional, transformative experiences, and researching them more, may give us a richer and more diverse picture of the 'religious' life of contemporary society than we currently have.

And what, then, of traditional forms of religion? As the argument in this book has developed it has become clear that I see the 'Generation X' search for meaning as being one that places a higher value on lived experience than on abstract concepts, that judges ideas about the world on what feels personally authentic rather than by deferring to some external authority, and that values the physical and non-verbal as much (if not sometimes more) than the cerebral and the verbal as a source of meaning in life. If I am right in making these claims, then it would seem that at least some sections of the Christian Church are in danger of alienating further those involved in this kind of pursuit of personal meaning. By this I am referring to the idea that is evident in some parts of the Church that the best response to its declining membership is to reassert vigorously 'traditional' or 'biblical' Christian doctrines and values. Whilst this assertion of a fixed set of doctrines and attitudes may draw some new people into the Church and may provide a sense of energy and purpose to some who remain members of it, this is likely to be perceived as unhelpful or irrelevant to those with a 'Generation X' view of life. The 'Generation X' search for meaning is not one that will be helped by religious institutions that seek to induct individuals into a predetermined set of religious ideas and attitudes (however innovative the manner in which these ideas are communicated and presented). Rather those with a 'Generation X' view of life are more likely to be drawn to groups and situations in which diverse, personal experience is recognised and valued, and in which they have some opportunity to gain an experience of a reality greater than their individual lives. Religious groups which function on the basis of fixed ideas and attitudes towards the world are less able to provide an environment in which individuals can speak and reflect freely about the meaning of their experience. Yet, I do not think that the Christian Church has nothing to offer to the 'Generation X' search for meaning. Indeed, in its traditions of mysticism, spiritual direction and contemplative prayer, the Church has potentially important and relevant resources for helping people reflect on and experience the reality beyond their individual lives.

We are standing at a crossroads in Western culture. Traditional religious institutions are in decline, and it is hard to imagine that we will ever see the majority of people in Western societies actively involved in such institutions again. As the membership and influence of these institutions weakens, we are in danger of losing sight of what forms 'religion' or the pursuit of meaning is taking in the contemporary world. And to lose sight of our need to find meaning, or of how we might be able to find meaning in life, carries severe risks for our well-being and our ability to resist unhealthy attitudes and lifestyles encouraged by an increasingly McDonaldized culture. This book has attempted to offer some, albeit very limited, signposts as to the direction that the contemporary search for meaning is taking. I hope it can be part of a growing, and increasingly well-informed discussion, in which we can learn more about the ways we are trying to find meaning in life, and to discuss critically what beliefs, resources and practices are more likely to help us live meaningfully and constructively. If we are indeed moving into a world in which we are living after religion, then we are moving into new territory. If nothing else, this book is an invitation for us to go on working on creating maps that will help us understand this new world in which we live.

NOTES

1 After Religion

1. Prof. Steve Bruce, 'The Future of Liberal Christianity', presentation made at the British Sociological Association Sociology of Religion conference held at Exeter University in March, 1999.
2. Numbers of people usually attending church in 1979 were 5,441,000. By 1989 this figure had dropped by around 700,000 to 4,742,800. Between 1989 to 1998, however, this figure dropped by nearly a million people to 3,714,700. As a percentage of the overall British population, those attending church regularly made up 11.7% of the population in 1979, 9.9% of the population in 1989, and 7.5% of the population in 1998.
3. An even more striking statistic from the church attendance survey is that, in 1989, 14% of British children aged 15 or under attended church regularly. By 1998, this figure had fallen to 8%.

2 Will the Real 'Generation X' Please Stand Up?

1. Mahedy and Bernadi (1994) actually claim that the degree of trauma experience by members of 'Generation X' is such that much of this generation demonstrates a similar level of traumatisation to that of Vietnam veterans.
2. On the basis of their research in youth culture, Furlong and Cartmel (1997) have argued that the lifestyles and choices one pursues remain very much limited by one's gender, ethnicity and social class. The culture of late modernity may therefore appear to offer greater freedom for defining the meaning and direction of one's own life, but this freedom may in reality only be experienced by certain people within Western society.
3. Matthew Guest has made the very reasonable suggestion to me that a further possible explanation for the growth of the concept 'Generation X' in the 1990s is precisely because it can be used by people in the reflexive construction of their identity. For example, by understanding myself as part of a wider generation with a particular outlook in life, I am therefore able to make some sense of particular attitudes or beliefs that I have (e.g. 'I feel suspicious about religious institutions – but then, after all, that's a typical GenX trait').

3   Flat-pack Furniture and Meccano Sets: 'Generation X' and Evangelical Christianity

1. I therefore think it is a mistake to classify the Mosaic church as a form of 'GenX' religion as Flory and Miller (2000) do. I would argue that the fact that Flory and Miller define 'Generation X' as those people who were born between 1961 and 1981 leads them to emphasise the similarities between young adult religious groups and to fail to observe the much more significant differences between them. The Mosaic church may indeed use multimedia resources, just as post-evangelical alternative worship services do, but the assumptions underlying the use of these resources are very different between these two groups.

4   'MTV Is My Bible . . .'

1. Brierley estimates that in 2000 there were 52,400 Buddhists, 675,000 Muslims and 400,000 Sikhs in Britain.
2. For the purposes of this book I am assuming a definition of popular culture as a set of practices and resources that are widely available and utilised within a particular cultural setting. I share the view of Forbes (2000) that it can be helpful to think of popular culture in contrast to 'high culture' (e.g. opera, traditional forms of art appreciation) and 'folk culture' (e.g. local musical forms, customs or legends often passed on by oral tradition). In contrast to 'high' and 'folk' culture, popular culture tends to be the cultural forms and practices that are widespread with a given society and is typically the focus and content of the mass media
3. Muggleton's (2000) research into the significance of 'sub-cultures' further illustrates the point that our sense of meaning is not passively assimilated from the cultures around us, but is actively and subjectively constructed from cultural symbols, practices and products.
4. It is important to retain some balance, however, and not to imagine that we are wholly uninfluenced by the world of meaning that a film/text seeks to construct. The cultural critic, bell hooks (1996), makes the point that we are attracted by film precisely because, for a period of time, we lose ourselves in its narrative and it is whilst we are immersed in its story that we can unconsciously assume something of the way in which the world is constructed within it. From the discussion in this chapter, it is clear though that we still do retain considerable freedom to challenge or adapt the meanings that we are presented with through popular culture.

5   Is There a 'Clubbing Spirituality'?

1. This point reflects a more general tension in the field of cultural studies between researchers who tend to offer theoretical analyses of popular cultural texts or events, and researchers who argue that to understand what meaning popular culture really has for people it is necessary to interview people or engage in some other kind of empirical research with them (see, e.g., Gray, 2002).

2. The interviews with clubbers included in this chapter are taken from a small-scale qualitative research study that I undertook exploring the significance that clubbing had for a small sample of young people. I conducted semi-structured interviews with 7 different people from the ages of 19–34 who identified clubbing as being an important part of their lives and who were regularly attending clubbing events. These interviews sought to understand what meaning and value clubbing held for each of these individuals, and the extent to which they perceived clubbing to have a spiritual or religious significance. The small nature of the sample clearly means that it is not possible to make more general claims about clubbers' attitudes on the basis of these interviews, but the interviews do help to illustrate the very diverse ways in which individuals can make sense of their clubbing experiences. The names used for these interviewees in this chapter are psuedonyms.

3. One of the limitations of these interviews that I recognised retrospectively was that they involved people who attended clubs that played a range of music from R'n'B, through UK Garage, to House and Trance/Techno. Not all of the participants used recreational drugs either. At this stage, I would speculate that there might be a slightly greater degree of agreement about the meaning of clubbing experiences amongst people who attend the same clubs or who use the same kinds of recreational drugs. For a study more focused around the use of a particular recreational drug, see Hammersley et al, 2002.

6   Surprising Moments of Grace: Douglas Coupland and a 'Generation X' Spirituality

1. Another recurrent motif in Coupland's novels is the complaint or anxiety that it is hard to shape the experiences of our lives into a single coherent story that makes sense of them (see, e.g., Coupland, 2001, p. 12).

2. Coupland therefore to a degree shares a similar notion to Beaudoin that popular culture can be mined as a source of meaning. However, Coupland seems much clearer than Beaudoin that this use of popular culture is an ironic activity (a way of marking time or making do) than something that reflects a serious belief that popular culture can provide us with a genuine sense of purpose in life.

7   Does 'Generation X' Need God?

1. Indeed research has frequently shown a positive correlation between religious faith and good levels of mental health (see Bergin and Richards, 1997), although the exact significance of this correlation is open to debate.

2. See, for example, the Christian mystic, Meister Eckhart who wrote about the 'Godhead behind God', the ultimate reality which is greater than, and which cannot be reduced to, any religious image or concept (see Davies, 1988).

BIBLIOGRAPHY

Alt.culture (2001) 'Generation X', downloaded from www.altculture.com on 13 April 2001.

Amoda (2001) *Moving into Ecstasy*, London, HarperCollins.

Awesomehouse (2002) 'The Matrix as Messiah movie', downloaded from www.awesomehouse.com/matrix/parallels.html on 19 January 2002.

Baker, J. (2000) 'Semiotic resistance – Coldcut in concert', unpublished paper.

Baker, J. (2001) 'Alternative worship and the significance of popular culture', downloaded from www.freshworship.org on 14 June 2001.

Barna Research Online (2002) 'Teenagers embrace religion but are not excited about Christianity, 10 January 2000', downloaded from www.barna.org/cgi-bin on 15 January 2002.

Bauman, Z. (2001) *Liquid Modernity*, Cambridge, Polity.

Beaudoin, T. (1998) *Virtual Faith*, Chichester, Jossey-Bass.

Bebbington, D. (1989) *Evangelicalism in Modern Britain*, London, Unwin Hyman.

Beck, U. (1992) *Risk Society: Towards a New Modernity*, London, Sage.

Beck, U., Giddens, A. and Lash, S. (1994) *Reflexive Modernization: Politics, Tradition and Aesthetics in the Modern Social Order*, Cambridge, Polity Press.

Bergin, A. and Richards, P. (1997) *A Spiritual Strategy for Counseling and Psychotherapy*, Washington, DC, American Psychological Association.

Bonacci, M. (1996) *We're on a Mission from God: The Generation X Guide to John Paul II, the Catholic Church and the Real Meaning of Life*, San Francisco, Ignatius Press.

Brierley, P. (1999) *UK Christian Handbook Religious Trends 2000/2001*, London, HarperCollins.

(2000) *The Tide is Running Out: What the English Church Attendance Survey Reveals*, London, Christian Research.

Bruce, S. (1995) *Religion in Modern Britain*, Oxford, Oxford University Press.

(1996) *Religion in the Modern World: From Cathedrals to Cults*, Oxford, Oxford University Press.

Bucknole, L. (2000) *The Long Weekend: A Decade of Club Culture*, documentary film submitted towards M. Phil. in History, Film and Television at the University of Birmingham.

Bullivant, C. (2001) 'Interview with Matt Redman', downloaded from www.soulsurvivor.com/uk/IMAG on 29 June 2001.

Caplow, T., Hout, M., Greeley, A., Woodberry, R., Hadaway, C., Marler, P. and Chaves, M. (1998) 'Exchange on church attendance in the United States', *American Sociological Review*, 63(1), pp. 112–30.

Collin, M. (1997) *Altered State*, London, Serpent's Tail.

Conn, D. (1997) *The Football Business: Fair Game in the 90s?* Edinburgh, Mainstream.

Coupland, D. (1992) *Generation X*, London, Abacus.

(1994) *Life After God*, London, Simon & Schuster.

(1998) *Girlfriend in a Coma*, London, Flamingo.

(2000) *Miss Wyoming*, London, Flamingo.

(2001) *All Families are Psychotic*, London, Flamingo.

(1995) 'Generation X'd', *Details*, June issue, p. 72 (obtainable via 'The Coupland File': www.geocities.com/SoHo/Gallery/5560/index.html).

Cox, K. (1998) *GenX and God: A GenX Perspective*, Chanhassen, Minn., Tekna Books.

Davie, G. (1994) *Religion in Britain Since 1945: Believing without Belonging*, Oxford, Blackwell.

Davies, O. (1988) *God Within: The Mystical Tradition of Northern Europe*, New York, Paulist Press.

de Certeau, M. (1984) *The Practice of Everyday Life*, Berkeley, University of California Press.

Drane, J. (1991) *What is the New Age Saying to the Church?* London, Marshall Pickering.

Flory, R. and Miller, D. (eds.) (2000) *GenX Religion*, New York, Routledge.

Forbes, B. (2000) 'Introduction', in B. Forbes and J. Mahan (eds.), *Religion and Popular Culture in America*, Berkeley, University of California Press, pp. 1–20.

Gallup (2002) 'Poll topics and trends – Religion', downloaded from www.gallup.com/poll/topics/religion2.asp on 15 January 2002.

Garratt, S. (1998) *Adventures in Wonderland: A Decade of Club Culture*, London, Headline.

Gergen, K. (1991) *The Saturated Self*, New York, Basic Books.

Gibbs, E. (2000) *ChurchNext: Quantum Changes in How We Do Ministry*, Downers Grove, Illinois, Inter-Varsity Press.

Giddens, A. (1991) *Modernity and Self-Identity: Self and Society in the Late Modern Age*, Cambridge, Polity.

Grace (2001) 'Welcome', downloaded from www.freshworship.org on 14 June 2001.

Gray, A. (2002) *Research Practice for Cultural Studies: Ethnographic Methods and Lived Cultures*, London, Sage.

Guest, M. (2002) ' "Alternative" worship: challenging the boundaries of the Christian faith', in E. Arweck and M. Stringer, *Theorising Faith: The Insider/Outsider Problem in the Study of Ritual*, Birmingham, University of Birmingham Press, pp. 35–56.

Hammersley, R., Khan, F. and Ditton, J. (2002) *Ecstasy and the Rise of the Chemical Generation*, London, Routledge.

Harrison, M. (1998) *High Society: The Real Voices of Club Culture*, London, Piatkus.

Haslam, D. (1997) 'DJ culture', in S. Redhead *et al.* (eds.), *The Clubculture's Reader*, Oxford, Blackwell, pp. 150–62.

Hay, D. (1982) *Exploring Inner Space: Scientists and Religious Experience*, Harmondsworth, Penguin.

(1990) *Religious Experience Today: Studying the Facts*, London, Mowbray.

Heathcote-James, E. (2001) *Seeing Angels*, London, Blake.

Heelas, P. (1996) *The New Age Movement*, Oxford, Blackwell.

Holtz, G. (1995) *Welcome to the Jungle: The Why Behind 'Generation X'*, New York, St Martin's Griffin.

Host (2001) 'about Host', downloaded from www.altworship.inuk.com on 29 June 2001.

Howe, N. and Strauss, B. (1993) *Thirteenth Gen: Abort, Retry, Ignore, Fail?* New York, Vintage Books.

hooks, b. (1996) *Reel to Real: Race, Sex and Class at the Movies*, London, Routledge.

Jenkins, H. (1992) *Textual Poachers: Television Fans and Participatory Culture*, New York, Routledge.

Klein, N. (2001) *No Logo*, London, Flamingo.

Laski, M. (1961) *Ecstasy: A Study of Some Secular and Religious Experiences*, London, Cresset Press.

Lyon, D. (1994) *Postmodernity*, Buckingham, Open University Press.

(2000) *Jesus in Disneyland: Religion in Postmodern Times*, Cambridge, Polity.

Lyotard, J.-F. (1984) *The Post-Modern Condition*, Manchester, Manchester University Press.

Mahedy, W. and Bernadi, J. (1994) *A Generation Alone: Xers Making a Place in the World*, Downers Grove, Illinois, IVP.

Malbon, B. (1999) *Clubbing: Dancing, Ecstasy and Vitality*, London, Routledge.

Marler, P. and Chaves, M. (1993) 'What the polls don't show: a closer look at U.S. church attendance', *American Sociological Review*, 58(6), pp. 741–52.

Marler, P. and Hadaway, C. (1999) 'Testing the attendance gap in a conservative church', *Sociology of Religion*, 60(2), pp. 175–86.

Marty, M. (1998) 'Revising the map of American religion', *The Annals of the American Academy of Political and Social Science*, July edition, pp. 13–27.

May, R. (1974) *Paulus: Reminiscences of a Friendship*, London, Collins.

Ministry of Sound (2000) 'Top UK dance acts set out to convert the US', downloaded from www.ministryofsound.co.uk/music/music_news.asp on 26 May 2000.

MORI (2001a) 'Paranormal survey conducted for the *Sun* between 4–5 February 1998', downloaded from www.mori.com/polls on 21 March 2001.

(2001b) '*Sunday Telegraph* Millennium Poll conducted on 19 December 1999', downloaded from www.mori.com/polls on 21 March 2001.

(2001c) 'Divine inspiration is our speciality! Poll for BBC Online conducted on 14th January 2000', downloaded from www.mori.com/polls on 21 March 2001.

Muggleton, D. (2000) *Inside Subculture: The Postmodern Meaning of Style*, Oxford, Berg.

News.bbc (2001) 'Christianity "almost vanquished" in the UK', downloaded from www.news.bbc.co.uk on 6 September 2001.

O'Rourke, P.J. (1994) *All the Trouble in the World*, London, Picador.

Pahl, R. (2001) *On Friendship*, Cambridge, Polity.

Parker, H., Aldridge, J. and Measham, F. (1998) *Illegal Leisure: The Normalization of Adolescent Recreational Drug Use*, London, Routledge.

Pauck, W. and Pauck, M. (1976) *Paul Tillich: His Life and Thought*, New York, Harper & Row.

Percy, M. and Taylor, R. (1997) 'Something for the weekend, sir? Leisure, ecstasy and identity in football and contemporary religion', *Leisure Studies*, 16, pp. 37–49.

Pilcher, J. (1995) *Age and Generation in Modern Britain*, Oxford, Oxford University Press.

Pinn, A. (1995) *Why, Lord? Suffering and Evil in Black Theology*, New York, Continuum.

Porterfield, A. (2001) *The Transformation of American Religion: The Story of a Late-Twentieth Century Awakening*, Oxford, Oxford University Press.

Prieto, L. (2000) 'An Urban Mosaic in Shangri-La', in R. Flory and D. Miller (eds.), *GenX Religion*, New York, Routledge, pp. 57–73.

Reifschneider, C. (1999) 'A new generation,' in A. Schieber and A. Olson (eds.), *What Next? Connecting Your Ministry with the Generation Formerly Known as X*, Minneapolis, Minn, Augsburg, pp. 17–40.

Radway, J. (1987) *Reading the Romance: Women, Patriarchy, and Popular Literature*, London, Verso.

Reynolds, S. (1998) *Energy Flash: A Journey Through Rave Music and Dance Culture*, London, Picador.

Riddell, M., Pierson, M. and Kirkpatrick, C. (2000) *The Prodigal Project: Journey into the Emerging Church*, London, SPCK.

Ritchie, K. (1995) *Marketing to Generation X*, New York, Free Press.

Ritzer, G. (1999) *Enchanting a Disenchanted World: Revolutionizing the Means of Consumption*, Thousand Oaks, California, Pine Forge Press.

(2000) *The McDonaldization of Society* (New Century Edition), Thousand Oaks, California, Pine Forge Press.

Roof, W. (1988) *American Mainline Religion: Its Changing Shape and Future*, New Brunswick, Rutgers University Press.

(1999) *Spiritual Marketplace: Baby Boomers and the Remaking of American Religion*, Princeton, NJ, Princeton University Press.

Rtts (2002) 'Intro', downloaded from www.rtts.com on 25 January 2002.

Rushkoff, D. (1996) *Playing the Future: What We Can Learn from the Digital Kids*, New York, Riverhead.

Sacks, P. (1996) *Generation X Goes to College*, Chicago, Open Court.

Sartre, J.-P. (1958) *Existentialism and Humanism*, London, Methuen.

Sartre, J.-P. (1958) *Being and Nothingness*, London, Routledge.

Saunders, N., Saunders, A. and Pauli, M. (2000) *In Search of the Ultimate High: Spiritual Experience Through Psychoactives*, London, Rider.

Saward, M. (1987) *Evangelicals on the Move*, London, Mowbray.

Schieber, A. and Olson, A. (eds.) (1999) *What Next? Connecting Your Ministry with the Generation Formerly Known as X*, Minneapolis, Minn, Augsburg.

Shepherd, N. (2001) 'Postmodern responses to being Church', downloaded from 'www.rbromley.org.uk/papers/postmodern_responses.htm' on 28 June 2001.

Silcott, M. (2000) *Rave America*, London, ECW Press.

Sim, S. (1999) *Derrida and the End of History*, Cambridge, Icon Books.

Soulcare (2002) 'Movie review: The Matrix (1999)', downloaded from www.soulcare.org/Matrix.html on 19 January 2002.

Soul Survivor (2001) 'Agony bloke, star letter – can I go clubbing?', downloaded from www.soulsurvivor.com/uk/IMAG/Content_Agony.asp on 29 June 2001.

Starkey, M. (1997) *God, Sex and Generation X*, London, Triangle.

Storey, J. (1999) *Cultural Consumption and Everyday Life*, London, Arnold.

Taylor, S. (1998) 'Partying like it's 1999', *The Observer*, 6 December, Features section, p. 5.

Theworldparty (2002) 'Homepage', downloaded from www.theworldparty.net on 24 January 2002.

Thornton, S. (1995) *Club Cultures: Music, Media and Subcultural Capital*, Cambridge, Polity.

Tidball, D. (1994) *Who are the Evangelicals? Tracing the Roots of Today's Movements*, London, Marshall Pickering.

Tillich, H. (1974) *From Time to Time*, London, George Allen & Unwin.

Tillich, P. (1949) *The Shaking of the Foundations*, London, Pelican.

—— (2000) *The Courage to Be* (2nd edition), New Haven, Yale University Press.

Tomlinson, D. (1995) *The Post-Evangelical*, London, Triangle.

Walker, A. (1998) *Restoring the Kingdom: The Radical Christianity of the House-Church Movement* (4th edition), Guildford, Eagle Press.

Walsch, N. (1997) *Conversations with God*, London, Hodder.

Ward, P. (1996) *Growing Up Evangelical: Youth-Work and the Making of a Subculture*, London, SPCK.

Wiethaus, U. (1996) *Ecstatic Transformation: Transpersonal Psychology in the Work of Mechtild of Magdeburg*, Syracuse, NY, Syracuse University Press.

Woodhead, L. and Heelas, P. (eds.) (2000) *Religion in Modern Times: An Interpretive Anthology*, Oxford, Blackwell.

Wynd (2002) 'Gnosticism reborn: The Matrix as shamanic journey', downloaded from www.wynd.org/matrix.htm on 19 January 2002.

Xenos (2002) 'Movie review: The Matrix', downloaded from www.xenos.org/ministries/crossroads/OnlineJournal/issue3/matrix.htm on 19 January 2002.

INDEX